Second Edition

Winning Words of Champions

Compiled by
Larry Bielat

**COACHES
≡ CHOICE™**

ISBN: 1-58518-880-8
Library of Congress Control Number: 2003115159
Book layout: Jeanne Hamilton
Cover design: Jeanne Hamilton

Coaches Choice
P.O. Box 1828
Monterey, CA 93942
www.coacheschoice.com

Dedication

To Lois, my wife

This is my beloved and this is my friend.
—Song of Solomon 5:16

Preface

Words, both written and spoken, have played an enormous role in the history of man. Some people have been gifted with the ability to put words into use that move others to great accomplishments.

Generals, presidents, teachers, philosophers, and coaches have had to call on words to inspire their charges. In this book, I have tried to organize, by subject, some of the quotes, poems, and one-liners that I have collected and found useful over the past 43 years as a coach, teacher, and father.

We frequently forget the power of words and use them to hurt rather than help. I hope my collection will be of some aid in the latter.

I would like to apologize to any originator to whom I have failed to give credit and to anyone who I gave credit not deserved.

Tiger Ellison delivered a speech to the National Football Coaches Association concerning, "Why Coach?" He closed with this poem, which sums up my feelings about this book.

An old man going a lone highway
Came at the evening cold and gray
To a chasm vast and deep and wide,
Through which was flowing a swollen tide.
The old man crossed in the twilight dim
That swollen stream held no fears for him
But he paused when safe on the other side
And built a bridge to span the tide.
"Old man," said a fellow pilgrim near,
"You are wasting strength and building here.
Your journey will end with the ending day;
You never again must pass this way.
You have crossed the chasm deep and wide;
Why build you the bridge at the eventide?"
The builder lifted his old gray head,
"Good friend, in the path I have come," he said,
"There followeth after me today
A youth whose feet must pass this way.
This swollen stream which has naught to me
To that fair haired youth may a pitfall be.
He, too, must cross in the twilight dim.
Good friend, I am building the bridge for him."

Contents

1

God

God never imposes a duty without giving time and strength to it.

Shift your sights from the superficial to the sacrificial. It's not your aptitude but your attitude, which will determine your altitude.

–Rev. Jesse Jackson

This quaint prayer hangs outside the door of the Refectory of the Cathedral at Chester, England.

Give me a good digestion, Lord,
And also something to digest;
Give me a healthy body, Lord,
With sense to keep it at its best.
Give me a healthy mind, Good Lord,
To keep the good and pure in sight,
Which, seeing sin, is not appalled
But finds a way to set it right.

Give me a mind that is not bored,
That does not whimper, whine, or sigh;
Don't let me worry over much
About the fussy thing called "I."
Give me a sense of humor, Lord,
Give me the grace to see a joke,
To get some pleasure out of life
And pass it on to other folk.

God Chooses Ordinary People for Extraordinary Work

Lord, help me to remember that nothing is going to happen to me today that You and I can't handle.

"*Belief* is the thermostat which regulates *success.*"

God's Hall of Fame

Your name may not appear down here
In this world's hall of fame.
In face you may be so unknown
That no one knows your name

The All Stars here may pass you by
On neon lights of blue,
But if you love and serve the Lord,
Then I have good news for you.

This hall of fame is only good
As long as time shall be,
But keep in mind God's hall of fame
Is for eternity.

To have your name inscribed up there
Is greater yet by far
Than all the halls of fame down here
And every man-made star.

This crowd on earth may soon forget
The heroes of the past.
They cheer like mad until you fall
And that's how long you last.

But God, he never does forget
And in His hall of fame,
By just believing in His son
Inscribed you'll find your name.

I tell you, friend, I wouldn't trade
My name however small,
That written there beyond the stars
In that celestial hall.

For any famous name on earth
Or glory that they share
I'd rather be an unknown here
And have my name up there.

Do you not know that you are God's temple and that God's spirit dwells in you?

−1 Cor. 3:16

An athlete is not crowned unless he competes according to the rules.

−2 Timothy 2:5

I can of mine ownself do nothing.

−John 5:30

You cannot love god without loving every fellow creature He made. An act of contempt or rejection or injustice or neglect toward the least, the lowest, the dumbest, the poorest—is an act against Him. If Christianity does not mean this, it means nothing.

When you're ready to quit and to give up the fight,
And the skies all above you are black as the night,
Then lift up your hand and through the owly night air,
There is power and triumph in confident prayer.

Do not pray for an easy life. Pray to be a *strong* person.

In a race, everyone runs but only one person gets the prize. So, run your race to win.

−1 Cor. 9:24

They who spend some time on their knees have no trouble standing on their feet.

"Character cannot be developed in ease and quiet. Only through experience of trial and suffering can the soul be strengthened, vision cleared, ambition inspired and success achieved. Silver is purified in fire and so are we. It is in the most trying times that our real character is shaped and revealed."

—Helen Keller

When a man has a great deal given to him, a great deal will be demanded of him.

–Luke 12:48

God, grant that I may live to fish until my dying day—And when it comes to my last cast, I then most humbly pray—When in the Lord's safe net I'm peacefully asleep, That in his mercy I be judged big enough to keep.

—A. Burham

Let us not pray to be sheltered from dangers but to be fearless when facing them.

Abraham Lincoln, during the darkest hours of the Civil War, in response to the question whether he was sure God was "on our side": "I do not know: I have not thought about that. But I am very anxious to know whether we are on *God's* side."

The Lord sometimes takes us into troubled waters not to drown but to cleanse us.

God's help is just a prayer away.

Dear Lord as we huddle here
Help us to see it clear,
That playing hard and playing fair,
Is what we are asking everywhere.

Dear Father,
Our one great coach, help us to play this game with dedicated spirit and willing body, with open and eager mind. So the lessons learned as we compete today may better prepare us for life's long way.

If you believe the Lord is directing your steps why try to understand everything that happens along the way?

My God is first, my team is second, and I am third.

Lord, when we are wrong, make us willing to change. And when we are right, make us easy to live with.

We can always "prove" that we are right, but is the Lord convinced?

Talent is God given—*Be Thankful*
Fame is man given—*Be Humble*
Conceit is self given—*Be Careful*

Do the very best you can, and leave the outcome to God.

Footprints

One night a man had a dream; he dreamed he was walking along the beach with the Lord.

Across the sky flashed scenes from his life. For each scene he noticed two sets of footprints in the sand—one belonging to him—the other belonging to the Lord.

When the last scene of his life flashed before him, he looked back at the footprints in the sane. He noticed that many times along the path of life there was only one set of footprints. He also noticed that it happened at the very lowest and saddest time in his life. This really bothered him and he questioned the Lord about it. "Lord, you said that once I decided to follow you, you would walk with me all the way. But, I have noticed that during the most troublesome times in my life there is only one set of footprints. I don't understand why, in times when I needed you most, you would leave me." The Lord replied, "My precious, precious child, I love you and I would never, never leave you during your times of trial and suffering. When you saw only one set of footprints, it was then that I carried you."

Take Time

Take Time to think—it is the source of power.
Take Time to play—it is the secret of youth.
Take Time to read—it is the foundation of wisdom.
Take Time to pray—it is the greatest power on earth.
Take Time to love and be loved—it is a God given privilege.
Take Time to be friendly—it is the road to happiness.
Take Time to laugh—it is the music of the soul.

The Committed Man—By Vince Lombardi

"We know how rough the road will be, how heavy here the load will be, we know about the barricades that wait along the track but we have set our soul ahead upon a certain goal ahead and nothing left from hell to sky shall ever turn us back."

I shall pass through this world but once. Any good that I can do, or any kindness that I can show any human being, let me do it now and not defer it, for I shall not pass this way again.

We were not put on this earth by God to make a *living* but to make a *life*.

"God will look us over not for medals, or diplomas, or degrees: BUT FOR SCARS"
–Edward Sheldon

God gave us two ends to use: one to think with—the other to sit with.
Success depends on which one you choose: heads you win, tails you'll lose.

What you are is God's gift to you—what you make of yourself is your gift to God.

"Climb 'Til Your Dream Comes True"

Often your tasks will be many, and more than you think you can do—
Often the road will be rugged and the hills insurmountable, too—
But always remember, the hills ahead are never as steep as they seem,
And with faith in your heart start upward and climb 'til you reach your dream.
For nothing in life that is worthy is ever too hard to achieve,
If you have the courage to try it and you have the faith to believe—
For faith is a force that is greater than knowledge or power or skill,
And many defeats turn to triumph if you trust in God's wisdom and will—
For faith is a mover of mountains, there's nothing that God cannot do—
So start out today with faith in your heart and "Climb 'til your dreams come true!"
–Helen Steiner Rice

A Man's Prayer—Grantland Rice

Let me live, oh Mighty Master, such a life as men shall know.
Tasting triumph and disaster, and not too much woe;
Let me run the gamut over, let me fight and love and laugh, and when I'm beneath the clover let this be my epitaph:
Here lies one who took his chances in the busy world of men; battled luck and circumstances fought and fell then fought again;
Won sometimes, but did no crowing; lost sometimes, but did not wail; took his beating, but kept going; never let his courage fail.
He was fallible and human, therefore loved and understood by his fellow man and woman, whether good or not so good;
Kept his spirit undiminished, never layed down on a friend, played the game till it was finished, lived a sportsman to the end…

Slow Me Down Lord

Slow me down Lord; ease the pounding of my heart by the quieting of my mind. Steady my hurried pace with a vision of the eternal reach of time.

Give me, amid the confusion of the day, the calmness of the everlasting hills. Break the tensions of my nerves and muscles with the soothing music of the singing streams that live in my memory, help me to know the magical, restoring power of sleep.

Teach me the art of taking minute vacations, of slowing down to look at a flower, to chat with a friend, to pat a dog, to read a few lines from a good book.

Slow me down Lord, and inspire me to send my roots deep into the soil of life's enduring values that I may grow toward the stars to my greater destiny.

In an age of false superlatives, we must remember that GOD alone is great

The Station

Tucked away in our subconscious is an idyllic vision. We see ourselves on a long trip that spans the continent. We are traveling by train. Out the windows, we drink in the passing scene of cars on nearby highways, of children waving at a crossing, of cattle grazing on a distant hillside, of smoke pouring from a power plant, of row upon row of corn and wheat, of flat lands and valleys, of mountains and rolling hillsides, of city skylines and village hills.

But uppermost in our minds is the final destination. On a certain day at a certain hour we will pull into the station. Bands will be playing and flags will be waving. Once we get there so many wonderful dreams will come true, and pieces of our lives will fit together like a completed jigsaw puzzle. How restlessly we paced the aisles, damning the minutes for loitering—waiting, waiting, waiting for the station.

"When we reach the station, that will be it," we cry. "When I'm 18, when I buy a new 450SL Mercedes Benz! When I put the last kid through college, when I reach the age of retirement, I shall live happily ever after!"

Sooner or later we must realize there is no station, no one place to arrive at once and for all. The true joy of life is the trip. The station is only a dream. It constantly outdistances us."

"Relish the moment" is a good motto, especially when coupled with Psalm 118:24: "This is the day which the Lord hath made; we will rejoice and be glad in it." It isn't the burdens of today that drive men mad. It's the regrets over yesterday and the fear of tomorrow. Regret and fear are twin thieves that rob us of today.

So, stop pacing the aisles and counting the miles. Instead, climb more mountains, eat more ice cream, go barefoot more often, swim more rivers, watch more sunsets, laugh more, cry less. Life must be lived as we go along. The station will come soon enough.

God's Minute

I have only just a minute, only sixty seconds in it, forced upon me, can't refuse it, didn't seek it, didn't choose it, but it's up to me to use it.

It may suffer if I lose it, give account if I abuse it, just a tiny little minute, but eternity is in it.

Competition!

This kinda blows my brain apart, Lord. Is it wrong for me to ram my shoulder into a guy? To body-check him—hard? To slap away his best shot? Is it wrong, Lord, is it?

When we were kids, I tackled my brother in a backyard game. Years smaller than he, I grabbed his ankle and rode him 30 yards before I tripped him—Thunk!...into the hard November ground. He looked across at me, surprised. "Way to go kid," he grunted—and the rest of that day I was a tiger!

Couldn't competition be like that sometimes, Lord? Admiring the brother who outdoes you...but still fighting like crazy to win?

The Bible doesn't say much about sports. But Paul must have known about the Olympics, 'cause he said to run the race—run it to win!

Lord, I know how Paul wanted me to compete; to fight my laziness, my selfishness, my desire to quit, my tendency to shove God into a corner, and run my life my way.

Competition grinds away my complacency, it polishes and lifts—lifts me to heights I didn't think possible. Competition demands my best, and that is of You.

I don't have to hate the guy who beats me—I can admire his ability, if God is in me...

Must I envy every time someone paints a great painting, or makes an A or hits a home run? Or can I rejoice in their art, their intelligence, their power? I am a child of God, unique, loved. I don't have to be what they are!

The Bible tells me, "We are more than conquerors through Him who loved us." Your power, Lord, is that of a billion suns. Yet you live within me, telling me to love, even as I compete. Love people. Love You, as You love us, and died for us.

Help me take that to the ball field, Lord.

—Harold Myra

The most valuable gift you can give another is a good example.

A Football Coach's Prayer

I suppose I should ask for flashy backs whose hips are in constant swivel and whose speed and dash make people say, "Boy, they run to beat the Devil."

I ought to include a massive line with chassis like big Mack trucks, whose brute strength scares all opponents and drops them like sitting ducks.

I could ask for a team with precision, whose efforts would all honors take and also plead for a squad with brains who would never make a mistake.

But Lord, I am an understandable coach—the talent cannot be all mine—so if you give me the things I ask for, I'll never complain or whine.

Just give me a bunch of eager kids with the spirit to fight and win, who will battle as soon as they take the field and most of all will never give in!

"There are no great people in this world, only great challenges which ordinary people rise to meet."

When God measures an athlete he puts a tape around your heart not your waist.

To Sportsmen Who Love The Game
To sportsmen who love the game beyond all profit and fame.
I lift my glass. Here's to the creed of you, here's to the breed of you.
Here while the bugles call, here, where we rise and fall,
Here where we storm the wall, you paved the way.
Oh where the cannons roar, knowing the heart calls for,
You wrote the winning score, back in our day.

–Grantland Rice

"Thank God every morning when you get up that you have something to do which must be done, whether you like it or not. Being forced to do your best will breed in you temperance, self-control, diligence, strength of will, contentment, and a hundred other virtues which the idle never know."

A Sportsman's Prayer

Our Father,
As Jesus took the bread and broke it, took the cup of wine and poured it, so, also, He took the "Flesh" and wore it and played the game of life as a Christian athlete.

Lord, help us to be good winners as well as losers in the game of life. Let us not pray to be the pitcher, or for any prominent place in the line-up. Play us anywhere you need us. We ask only that you give us patience, courage, and stamina to give You the best we've got in the game.

If we wind up as the catcher, and many bad hops, wild pitches, and foul tips come our way, may we not complain, nor alibi, nor protest that the game was a frame-up. Let us never side-step one that is too hot to handle.

Lord, if we turn out to be the hitting star, keep us humble in heart.

Please play us wherever You will in such a way that You will have no regrets for having given us the chance.

And finally, dear Lord, when we reach that "last big inning" and the evening shadows are falling across home plate may we not have to "slide in" nor be squeezed in." But grant that we will get that last big hit and trot safely home.

–C. Wesley Grisham

Anger is more often harmful than the injury that caused it.

Where GOD has put a period, don't change it to a question mark.

Found on the Body of a Confederate Soldier

"I asked for strength—that I might achieve.
He made me weak—that I might obey.
I asked for health—that I might do greater things.
I was given grace—that I might do better things.
I asked for riches—that I might be happy.
I was given poverty—that I might be wise.
I asked for power—that I might have the praise of men.
I was given weakness—that I might feel the need of God.
I asked for all things that I might enjoy life.
I was given life—that I might enjoy all things.
I received nothing that I asked for—and all that I hoped for.
My prayer was answered."

Understanding

Not more of light I ask, O God,
But eyes to see what is;
Not sweeter songs, but ears to hear
The present melodies;
Not more of strength, but how to use
The power that I possess;
Not more of love, but skill to turn
A frown to a caress;
Not more of joy, but how to feel
Its kindly presence near
To give to others all I have
Of courage and of cheer.
No other gifts, dear God, I ask,
But only sense to see
How best these precious gifts to use
Thou hast bestowed on me.
Help me to move the slow of spirit
By some clear, winning word of love;
Teach me to stay the wayward feet
And guide them in the homeward way.

A Coach's Prayer

Help me to understand my players, their strengths and weaknesses, to treat them in such a way as to smooth their rough spots, and polish their strong traits. During this quest, O Lord, make me as demanding of myself as I am of them. Give me the courage to realize my mistakes and not knowingly commit them again.

May I not play a seriously injured athlete. Forbid that I should laugh at their mistakes, to resort to sadism and ridicule as punishment. Let me not tempt a player to play dirty or illegal. So guide me game to game that I may demonstrate by all I say and do that maintaining training rules, hard work, and personal dedication are the ingredients of athletic success.

Reduce, I pray, vanity in me. May I cease to nag; and when we have lost, help me, O Lord, to hold my tongue.

Blind me to the small errors of my players and help me to see the good things that they do. Give me a ready word of honest praise.

Help me to treat my players as young adults and not like little children; yet let me not expect of them the performance of adults. Let me not expect of them things that are impossible nor less of them than is possible. Guide me along those paths that will lead each player as close to his or her potential as is possible.

Forbid that I should ever punish them for falling short while trying their hardest. Grant that I may direct them to those experiences that will make of them better persons and have the courage always to withhold experiences which I know will do them harm.

Make me so fair and just, considerate and understanding of my players that they may have genuine respect for me. Fit me to be the best example that is within me to be.

With all thy gifts, O God, give me poise, patience, and humility.

God never sends the winter
Without the joy of spring,
And though today your heart may cry,
Tomorrow it will SING!

The Self Esteem Credo

God made me—I was no accident, no happenstance. I was in God's plan, and He doesn't make junk. I was born to be a successful human being; I am somebody special, unique, definitely one of a kind, and I love me.

That is essential, so that I might love others also. I have talents and potential. Yes, there is greatness in me, and if I harness my special qualities, then I will write my name in the sands of time with my deeds.

Yes, I must work hard and long, and with great drive if I am to excel. I will pay that price. Talents demand daily care and honing. I was born in God's image and likeness. I will strive to do God's will.

"Don't bother to give God instructions; just report for duty!"

Doubt sees the obstacles
Faith sees the way
Doubt sees the darkest night
Faith sees the day
Doubt dreads to take a step
Faith soars on high
Doubt questions, "Who believes?"
Faith answers "I."

I really don't have goals to be the greatest coach in the business. I just try to achieve the best with the talent God has given me. If I do that, I'm satisfied.
—Tom Landry, Dallas Cowboys

That which does not begin with *God* ends in failure.

A Daily Dozen

Believe in yourself, for you are marvelously endowed.

Believe in your job, for all honest work is sacred.

Believe in this day, for every minute contains an opportunity to do good.

Believe in your family, and create harmony by trust and cooperation.

Believe in your neighbor, for the more friends you can make, the happier you will be.

Believe in uprightness, for you cannot go wrong doing right.

Believe in your decisions; consult God first, then go ahead.

Believe in your health; stop taking your pulse, etc., etc.

Believe in your church; you encourage others to attend by attending yourself.

Believe in the now; yesterday is past recall, and tomorrow may never come.

Believe in God's promises; He means it when He says, "I am with you always."

Believe in God's mercy; if God forgives you, you can forgive yourself and try again tomorrow.

—Alastair MacOdrum

The difficulties of life are meant to make us better not bitter.

Faith is like radar that perceives through the fog the reality of things at a distance that the human eye cannot see.

—Corrie Ten Boom

Not to decide is to decide.

"We cannot get away from God, although we can ignore Him."

—James Cabot

Young and Wishing

God in heaven, I am young, and don't understand what it is like to be a parent. It must be very hard, since so many people are failing at it these days.

I pray for Mom and Dad, God, that you will help them to be good parents; strong in the ways you want them to be, so I can look up to them with admiration and feel confident that their instruction is right.

Help me Dear Lord, to understand my parents. Remind me that when I don't get my way it is because they love me and not because they want to be mean or deprive me of anything.

Put in my heart the respect and consideration they deserve for their years of hard work and sacrifice. They raised me the best way they know how. Let me not repay them with grief or shame. Rather help me to give them obedience, respect, forgiveness and love. Most of all, God, while I still have them here on earth, help me to appreciate my parents.

Prayers Can't be Answered
Unless They are Prayed...

Life without a purpose is barren indeed.
There can't be a harvest unless you plant seed;
There can't be attainment unless there's a goal,
And man's but a robot unless there's a soul
If we send no ships out, no ships will come in,
And unless there's a contest, nobody can win.
For games can't be won unless they are played,
And prayers can't be answered unless they are prayed.
So, whatever is wrong with your life today,
You'll find a solution if you kneel down and pray,
Not just for pleasure, enjoyment, and health,
Not just for honors and prestige and wealth.
For great is your gladness and rich your reward
When you make your life's purpose the choice of the Lord.
–Helen Steiner-Rice

Dear God,
Help me to be a good sport in this game of life. I don't ask for an easy place in the line-up. Put me anywhere you need me. I only ask that I can give you 100% of all I have. If all the hard knocks seem to come my way, I thank you for the compliment. Please help me to remember that you'll never send more trouble to me than I can handle.

Help me, O Lord, to accept the bad breaks as part of the game.

No matter what the others do, help me to be strong mentally and to never give up, regardless of the task. Let me not complain, nor find fault, nor be envious of another's success. Help me to be a good coach and to be a good example for the young people I work with.

Thank you God, for giving me the enthusiasm and confidence necessary to do my job well. Thank you, also, for my health, my family, and for all the goodness you've shown me here on earth.

Finally, God, if the natural course of events turns against me, help me to accept that as part of the game, too. All that I want is to believe in my heart that I played this game of life as well as I could, and that I didn't let you down.

–Chaplain's Digest

Dear Lord,
In the Battle that goes on for life, I ask for a field that is fair, a Chance that is equal with all in strife, The Courage to do and dare.

If I should win, let it be by the code, my faith and my honor held very high. If I should lose, let me stand by the road and cheer as the winner rides by.

–Knute Rockne

God gives us the ingredients for our daily bread, but He expects us to bake it.

If God Would Go on Strike

It's just a good thing that God Above
Has never gone on strike
Because He wasn't treated fair
For things He didn't like.
If He ever once sat down and said
"That's it, I'm through;
I've had enough of those on earth
So this is what I'll do,
I'll give my orders to the Sun,
Cut off your heat supply.
And to the moon, give no more light.
And run the ocean dry,
Then just to really make it tough
And put the pressure on
Turn off the air and oxygen
'Til every breath is gone."
Do you know He'd be justified
If fairness was the game,
For no one has been more abused
Or treated with disdain
We say we want a better deal;
And so on strike we go,
But what a deal we've given God,
To whom everything we owe.
We don't care who we hurt or harm
To gain the things we like,
But what a mess we'd all be in
If God would go on strike.

Maybe the Lord lets some people get into trouble because that is the only time they ever think of Him.

Use everything as if it belongs to God. It does.

God did not write solo parts for very many of us. He expects us to be participants in the great symphony of life

–Donald Tippett

"Jesus always followed what most interested the people. He talked about the lessons found in everyday life. You can be sure He would find many lessons in American sports. He taught all the qualities that make for good sports: discipline, courage, health, cleanliness, and mental awareness."

—Dr. Norman Vincent Peale

One Solitary Life

Here is a young man who was born in an obscure village, the child of a peasant woman. He grew up in another village. He worked in a carpenter shop until he was thirty, and then for three years he was an itinerant preacher. He never wrote a book. He never held an office. He never owned a home. He never had a family. He never went to college. He never put his foot inside a big city. He never traveled 200 miles from the place where he was born. He never did one of the things that usually accompany greatness. He had no credentials but himself.

While he was still a young man, the tide of public opinion turned against him. His friends ray away. He was turned over to his enemies. He went through the mockery of a trial. He was nailed to a cross between two thieves. While he was dying, his executioners gambled for the only piece of property he had on earth, and that was his coat. When he was dead, he was laid in a borrowed grave through the pity of a friend.

Nineteen centuries have come and gone, and today he is the central figure of the human race and the leader of the column of progress. All the armies that ever marched and all the kings that ever reigned have not affected the life of man upon this earth as has that one solitary life.

God hath entrusted me with myself.

Be Yourself—but be your best self. Dare to be different and to follow your own star.

And don't be afraid to be happy. Enjoy what is beautiful. Love with all your heart and soul. Believe that those you love, love you.

Forget what you have done for your friends, and remember what they have done for you. Disregard what the world owes you, and concentrate on what you owe the world.

When you are faced with a decision, make that decision as wisely as possible and then forget it. The moment of absolute certainty never arrives.

Above all, remember that God helps those who help themselves. Act as if everything depended on you, and pray as if everything depended on God.

—S. H. Phayer

Football Players Prayer

Oh Mighty God, our coach supreme, Help me train to make your team.
Help me to play by rules of Thine
And guide me through temptation's line.
Give me a berth upon your squad,
Make me all-conference on the team of God.
Help me to block all that is wrong,
Lend me Thy strength, make my tackles strong.
Please, help me play in life's football game.
And, most gracious Lord, help my teammates the same.

A Coaches Reward

A man knocked at the Heavenly Gate, his face looked tired and old.
He stood before the man of fate, for admission to the fold.
"What have you don't," St. Peter asked, "To gain admission here?"
"I've worked as a coach for many and many a year."
The Pearly Gate swung open wide, St. Peter rang the bell.
"Come in, come in and choose your harp, you've had your share of Hell."

Coach's Prayer of Thanks...

Dear God,

Thank you for the opportunities and challenges you have blessed us with. Help us to love our moms and dads, our families, our friends, relatives, and teammates as you love us.

Help us to sacrifice our personal welfare for others as you did for us; and help us to utilize our athletic abilities to glorify Your name.

For it is only in giving that we emulate You. I pray that we may always be true sportsmen on the gridiron of life.

May we learn to obey life's rules so that we may be spared its harsh penalties;

Learn to prize honest defeat above a dishonest victory; Be brave in defeat, humble in victory.

When we strive to become better athletes, may these conversion attempts succeed.

May we so play the game that the Divine Referee will include us in His Hall of Fame.

The Test...

There was a race and all of us ran.
The coach said, "Do the best you can."

We tried. We lost. One winner claimed
The prize at which we all had aimed.

Applause rang out, and then we knew
That it was meant for losers too.

O God, run with me in life's race,
Encourage me to seek first place.

But if I fail—Please, give me Grace
To see the goal I reach is best for me.

The joy of living comes from immersion in something that we know to be bigger, better, more during and worthier than we are.

The Cross in My Pocket

I carry a cross in my pocket
A simple reminder to me
Of the fact that I am a Christian
No matter where I may be

This little cross is not magic, nor
Is it a good luck charm
It isn't meant to protect me
From every physical harm

It's not for identification
For all the world to see
It's simply an understanding
Between my Savior and me

When I put my hand in my pocket
To bring out a coin or key
The cross is there to remind me
Of the price He paid for me

It reminds me too, to be thankful
For my blessings day by day
And to strive to serve Him better
In all that I do and say

It's also a daily reminder
Of the peace and comfort I share
With all who know my master
And give themselves to His care

So, I carry a cross in my pocket
Reminding no one but me
That Jesus Christ is Lord of my life
If only I'll let Him be

"When the one great scorer comes to mark against your name he writes—not that you won or lost—but *how* you played the game."

—Grantland Rice

To Be Successful…

Don't worry when you are doing the best you know how to do.
Don't hurry when success depends on accuracy.
Don't believe a thing is impossible without trying it.
Don't imagine that good intentions are enough.
Don't think evil of a friend unless you have all the facts.
Don't harbor bitterness in your soul overnight.

Thank you, God, for little things that often come our way. The things we take for granted but don't mention when we pray. The unexpected courtesy, the thoughtful, kindly deed. A hand stretched out to help us in the time of sudden need. O make us more aware, dear God, of little daily graces that come to us with 'sweet surprise' from never-dreamed-of places.

It Can't Be True

I've heard it said the world's a dismal place. But I know better…for I have seen the dawn and walked in the splendor of a morning's sun…blinked at the brilliance of the dew and beheld the gold and crimson of an autumn landscape.

I've heard it said the world is sad. I can't agree…for I have heard the cheerful songs of feathered masters…heard the low laughter of the leaves and the everlasting chuckle of a mountain brook.

I've heard it said the world's a place of musty, sordid things. It can't be true…for I have seen the rain…watched it bathe the earth, the very air…and I have seen the sky, newly scrubbed and spotless, blue from end to end…and I've watched the winter's snow drape tree and bush, to look like Nature's freshly laundered linen hung to dry.

I've heard it said the world is evil, but they are wrong…For I have known its people…watched them die to save a freedom, bleed to save a life…spend of themselves to stem disaster, of their wealth to ease distress…and I have watched them live, love, and labor…watched them hope, dream, and pray, side by side.

I've heard them say these things, but I would disagree…because for every shadow, I have seen one hundred rays of light…for every plaintive note, I've heard a symphony of joy…for every pennyweight of bad, I have found a ton of good…and I thank God I belong.

An Athlete's Prayer

Help me to play the game, dear Lord, with all my might and main; Grant me the courage born of right, a heart to stand the strain…

Send me a sense of humor, Lord, to laugh when victory's mine—To laugh, if I should meet defeat, without a fret or whine…

Give me the grace to follow rules, to 'fess up when I'm wrong. When silence or some other thing wins plaudits from the throng…

When foes are tough and fighting fierce and I am getting weak, Dear God, don't ever let me show a broad, bright, yellow streak.

And teach me, Lord, life's game to play just one day at a time. With Thee as coach and trainer, Lord, real victory must be mine.

Ten Reasons Why I Swear

It pleases my parents so much.

It is a fine mark of coolness.

It proves I have self-control.

It indicates how clearly my mind operates.

It makes my conversation so pleasing to everyone.

It leaves no doubt in anyone's mind as to my bringing up.

It impresses people that I have more than an ordinary education.

It is an unmistakable sign of culture and refinement.

It makes me a very desirable personality among others and respectable in society.

It is my way of honoring God who said. "Thou shalt not take the name of the Lord thy God in vain."

I am neither good nor bad, I am both. I am neither honest nor dishonest, I am both. I am neither generous nor selfish, I am both. I am neither happy nor sad, I am both. But God accepts me, forgives me, and loves me, and I now accept, forgive, and love myself.

The Greatest Coach of All Time
by Football Coach Steve Sloan

At the end of time God appointed a committee headed by Saint Paul to determine who was the greatest coach of all time. God wanted this information so he could appoint an athletic director for all sports in Heaven. These things were decided upon at the first committee meeting:

That a coach's won-loss record would not be a factor in the decision.

Honors received by the coach would not be a factor.

Amount of money made by the coach would not be a factor.

Number of clinics spoken to would not be a factor.

Number of All-Conference or All American players produced would not be a factor.

Number of national or state championships would not be a factor.

Number of golf or tennis tournaments played in would not be a factor.

Number of assistants who became head coaches would not be a factor.

Amount of stock would not be a factor.

Square footage in the coach's house would not be a factor.

The committee chose the greatest coach of all time by one criterion—the greatest genuine depth of love for his or her players. Strangely enough, the winner was a high school coach somewhere in Montana whom God subsequently appointed Athletic Director for Heaven with an eternal contract.

2

Character
❖
Discipline
❖
Pride

*Your character is what you have left when you
have lost everything else you can possibly lose.*

Photo: Donald Miralle/Getty Images

A coach's true value, and that of sport, is ultimately measured by what was learned rather than what was won.

—Bill Ellias Jr.

Pride...

- All athletes who work toward athletic excellence equate self-control with pride.
- When we say of people that they have pride, we mean they have a degree of willpower, concentration, and mental toughness that permits them to overcome temptations toward negative attitudes and behaviors.
- There is a high correlation between self-control (pride) and athletic success.
- Research clearly shows that self-control, mental toughness, and trust are the leading three attributes that distinguish the highly competitive from the marginal athlete.
- Quote: "Competitors who know what they should do are far more numerous than those who do what they should."
- The self-image must be resistant to embarrassment, depression, tension, distractions, and temptations.
- Neither the opponent's success nor one's own failure is intimidating.
- The athlete who is best controlled, mentally prepared, and physically toned—who has the most pride wins.

People are not *excellent* because they achieve great things; they achieve great things because they choose to be *excellent*.

Don't look for miracles. You are a miracle.

If what you did yesterday still looks big to you, you haven't done much today.

Prudence—the ability to regulate and discipline one's self through the exercise of reason.

Fortitude—the endurance of physical or mental hardships or suffering without giving way under strain. It is firmness of mind in meeting danger or adversity; resolute endurance; courage and staying power. It is the possession of the stamina essential to face that which repels or frightens one, or to put up with the hardships of a job imposed. It implies triumph. Synonyms are grit, backbone, pluck, and guts.

Temperance—habitual moderation in the indulgence of appetites and passions.

Justice—the principle of rectitude and just dealing of humans with each other; also conformity to it; integrity.

Faith—trust in God.

Hope—the desire with expectation of obtaining what is desired, or belief that it is obtainable.

Charity—the act of loving all people because they are children of God. It stresses benevolence and goodwill in giving and in the broad understanding of others with kindly tolerance.

I am only one, but I am one. I can't do everything but I can do something, and that which I can do, I ought to do, and that which I ought to do by God's grace, I shall do…

Character is made by what you stand for; reputation by what you fall for.

Would the kid you were be proud of the adult you are?

If you fail to teach your children respect for others, you and not they are responsible for their actions.

Don't look for an answer to your problem;
Look for lots of answers, then choose the best one.

The time to have "second thoughts" is before you make decisions, not after.

Maturity

Maturity is the ability to base a judgment on the big picture…the long haul.

Maturity is the ability to stick with a project or situation until it is finished.

Maturity is the ability to face unpleasantness, frustration, discomfort, and defeat without complaint or collapse.

Maturity is the ability to live up to your responsibilities and this means being dependable, keeping your word. The world is filled with people who can't be counted on. People who never seem to come through in the clutches. People who break promises.

Maturity is the ability to make a decision and stand by it.

Maturity is the ability to harness your abilities and energies.

You don't win football games on optimism. You win with preparation.
—Monte Clark

Are you trying to make something *for* yourself or something *of* yourself?

Some athletes are bigger, faster, stronger, and smarter than others—but not a single person has a corner on dreams, desire, or ambition.

–Duffy Daugherty

They who cannot forgive, destroy the bridge over which they may one day need to pass.

Do all the good you can by all the means you can in all the ways you can, in all the places you can at all the times you can to all the people you can as long as you can…

There is no right way to do the wrong thing.

Silence is not always golden…sometimes it is just plain yellow.

It is better to keep your mouth shut and be thought a fool, than to open it and remove all doubt.

Temper is what gets most of us in trouble.
Pride is what keeps us there.

One never discloses his own character so clearly as when he describes another's.

Failure to prepare certainly means preparing to *fail*.

–John Wooden

I would rather be disliked for what I am, than to be liked for what I am not.

Better a day of strife than a century of sleep.

As in nature, as in art, so in grace; it is rough treatment that gives souls, as well as stones, their luster. The more the diamond is cut the brighter it sparkles; and in what seems hard dealing, there God has no end in view but to perfect his people.

–K.S. Guthrie

There is no easy way.

The right angle to approach any problem is the TRY angle.

You never get a *second* chance to make a good *first* impression.

You can tell more about people by what they say about others…than you can by what others say about them.

Character is the result of two things: mental attitude and the way we spend our time.

–Elbert Hoggard

You are the one who has to decide whether you'll do it or toss it aside. You are the one who makes up your mind whether you'll lead or linger behind—whether you'll try for the goal that's afar or be contended to stay where you are. Take it or leave it. Here's something to do—just think it over. It's all up to you! What do you wish? To be known as a good person who's willing to work, scorned for a loaner or praised by your chief, rich or poor or beggar or thief? Eager or earnest or dull through the day, honest or crooked? It's you who must say! You must decide in the face of the test whether you'll shirk it or give it your best.

Who gossips to you will gossip of you.

Don't belittle…*be big*

Swearing is a device for making ignorance audible!

–Mel Johnson

Make your opponent *fear* and *respect* you.

This is a final test of a gentleman: His respect for those who can be of no possible service to him.

–Phelps

Talent will get you to the top but it takes character to keep you there. –John Wooden

Play for more than you can afford to lose, and you will learn the game.

If you don't take the time to find out what you're all about, you'll never know what life is all about.

No price it too high to pay for a good reputation.

Let everyone sweep in front of their own door and the whole world will be clean.

The bigger a person's head gets, the easier it is to fill their shoes.

Pride…character…work habits…lead to success.

–Rick Comley

The measure of a man's real character is what he would do if he knew he never would be found out.

–T.B. Macaulay

Eat to live not live to eat.

It is my belief that *discipline*, well-earned *pride*, and a high-degree of *unselfishness* contribute to achieving a desirable morale...the most important element in a successful team.

–John Majors

The great thing in this world is not so much where we are, but in what direction we are moving.

–O.W. Holmes

The person who properly disciplines himself to do those things that he does not especially care to do, becomes successful.

–Frank Leahy

Some folks stay right in the rut while others head the throng.
All people may be born quite equal but—they don't stay that way long.
There is many a person with a gallant air, goes galloping to the fray;
But the valuable one is the one who's there when the smoke has cleared away.
Some "don't get nuthin' out of life" but when their whines begin,
We often can remind them that they "don't put nuthin' in."

It is more important to know where you are going than to get there quickly.
–M. Newcomber

Before you flare up at anyone's faults, take time to count 10, *10 of your own*.

Resolutions

No one will get out of this world alive. Resolve therefore in the year to maintain a sense of values.

Take care of yourself. Good health is everyone's major source of wealth.

Without it, happiness is almost impossible. Resolve to be cheerful and helpful. Avoid angry, abrasive persons. They are generally vengeful. Avoid zealots. They are generally humorless. Resolve to listen more and talk less. No one ever learns anything by talking. Be leery of giving advice. Wise folks don't need it, and fools won't heed it.

Resolve to be tender with the young, compassionate with the aged, sympathetic with the striving, and tolerant of the weak and the wrong. Sometimes in life you will have been all of these.

Do not equate money with success. There are many successful moneymakers who are miserable failures as human beings. What counts most about success is how one achieves it.

Resolve to love, next year, someone you didn't love this year. Love is the most enriching ingredient of life.

Playin' Square

Don't count the game as lost, my child, because the runs are more for the opposing team than yours. What matter is the score? Why, being beaten can't impair your courage when you're playin' square. When bigger game and bigger stakes are yours to lose and win, don't waste your time connivin' for advantage—just dig in. And do your best to claim your share; But first be sure you're playin' square.

—Jos. R. Cushing

Character is a conquest, *not a bequest.*

Three Kinds of Athletes

On all squads there are three kinds of athletes.

First, there is the athlete who is a help. This is the one who takes a keen interest in the whole concern. He or she feels a part of the set-up, and takes pride in it. Every now and then he or she suggests some improvement. Often he or she does more than is expected. When given a job to do, he or she does not enlarge on the difficulties or the responsibility of it. He or she just pitches in and does it.

Second, there is the athlete who is a habit. A good worker, he or she takes an interest, more or less, in the job, but is seldom concerned in the least about the whole concern. He or she learned to do one thing, and do it reasonably well. Work is all a matter of habit. He or she hates to be shifted from one job to another. He or she lacks drive. He or she is good, but is nailed down to a routine, and sees anything outside that routine as a nuisance rather than an opportunity.

The third type of athlete is a hindrance. He or she is the one who dislikes his or her job. He or she does not want to work, and almost feels a grievance against anyone who gives him or her a chance to better his or her lot. He or she never has a good word for anyone or anything. He or she is strong on objecting, great on refusing, marvelous on criticizing, but weak on doing. He or she is against everything that spells an effort. He or she can't take it. He or she never takes correction in good spirit; instead, he or she walks off with a growl. He or she is an athlete who can never be promoted or advanced. He or she is a hindrance.

The person who gets ahead, is the one who does more than is necessary—and keeps on doing it.

Greatness cannot be achieved without *discipline*.

When a person is wrapped up in herself, she makes a pretty small package.

Character is what a person is in the dark.

Don't count the days, make the days count.

The real measure of an athlete is not what she is…but what she could be.

So live that you wouldn't be ashamed to sell the family parrot to the town gossip.

–Will Rogers

Inability to tell good from evil is the greatest worry of life.

–Cicero

The people most preoccupied with titles and status are usually the least deserving of them.

Discipline is the refining fire by which *talent* becomes *ability*.

–Roy Smith

Reputation is what others think you are.
Character is what God knows you are.

We Need People

...who cannot be bought...whose word is their bond.

...who put character above wealth.

...who possess opinions and a will.

...who are larger than their vocations.

...who do not hesitate to take chances.

...who will make no compromise with wrong.

...who will not lose their individuality in a crowd.

...who will be as honest in small things as in great things.

...who will not say they do it "because everybody else does it."

...whose ambitions are not confined to their own selfish desires.

...who give thirty-six inches to the yard and thirty-two quarts to the bushel.

...who will not have one brand of honesty for business purposes and another for private life.

...who are try to their friends through good report and evil report, in adversity as well as prosperity.

...who do not believe that shrewdness, sharpness, cunning, and long-headedness are the best qualities for winning success.

...who are not ashamed or afraid to stand for the truth when it is unpopular, who can say "no" with emphasis, although all the rest of the world says "yes."

–California Free Enterprise Association

Fame is a vapor, popularity an accident, riches take wings. Only one thing endures—character.

–Horace Greely

Character is much easier kept than recovered.

The Bench Warmer

The radio screams and the papers print reams for the player who carries the ball,

While never a word is written or heard of the players who sit through it all.

But there on the bench a dozen hearts wrench when a man goes in the fray.

They never go in, but they take it and grin—for them it's all work and no play.

When the vacant seats stare you will find them all there in the thick of the strife and the storm.

They are battered and bruised—it's for practice they're used in the game they just keep the bench warm.

So take off your hat to the players who sat through the Saturday afternoon game,

And remember that they had a part in the play

That to others brought glory and fame.

–C.J. Perkins

True greatness consists of being great in little things.

From Roses to Raspberries

The lad they are cheering with accents endearing, whose pathway is strewn with roses so red;

May boot one tomorrow and learn to his sorrow, that raspberries grow when roses are dead.

So a word of advice to the popular star, from roses to raspberries ain't very far.

Courage is the same size in any person.

The tougher the job the greater the reward.

The surest way not to fail, is to be determined to succeed.

What is Class?

Class never runs scared. It is surefooted and confident in the knowledge that you can meet life head on and handle whatever comes along.

Jacob had it. Esau didn't. Symbolically, we can look to Jacob's wrestling match with the angel. Those who have class have wrestled with their own personal "angel" and won a victory that marks them thereafter.

Class never makes excuses. It takes its lumps and learns from past mistakes.

Class is considerate of others. It knows that good manners are nothing more than a series of petty sacrifices.

Class bespeaks an aristocracy that has nothing to do with ancestors or money. The most affluent blueblood can be totally without class while the descendant of Welsh miners may ooze class from every pore.

Class never tries to build itself up by tearing others down. Class is ALREADY up and need not strive to look better by making others look worse.

Class can "walk with royalty and keep its virtue and talk with crowds and keep the common touch." Everyone is comfortable with people who have class—because they are comfortable with themselves.

If you have class you don't need much of anything else. If you don't have class, no matter what else you have—it doesn't make much difference.

The quitter gives an alibi,
The mongrel, he gets blue
The fighter goes down fighting,
But the thoroughbred comes thru.

Hustle: You can't survive without it.

Winning isn't everything, but wanting to win is.

Those with clenched fists cannot shake hands.

Give me an athlete who holds on when others let go, who pushes ahead when others turn back, who stiffens up when others retreat, who knows no such words as "can't" and "quit" and I'll show you someone who will win in the end.

Always remember—anything is yours if you are willing to pay the price.

Self-respect cannot be hunted. It cannot be purchased. It is never for sale. It cannot be fabricated out of public relations. It comes to us when we are alone, in quiet moments, in quiet places, when we suddenly realize that, knowing the good, we have done it; knowing the beautiful, we have served it; knowing the truth, we have spoken it.
—A. Witney Griswald

Be understanding to your enemies.

Be loyal to your friends.

Be strong enough to face the world each day.

Be weak enough to know you cannot do everything alone.

Be generous to those who need help.

Be frugal with what you need yourself.

Be wise enough to know that you do not know everything.

Be foolish enough to believe in miracles.

Be willing to share your joys.

Be willing to share the sorrow of others.

Be a leader when you see a path others have missed.

Be a follower when you are shrouded by the mists of uncertainty.

Be the first to congratulate an opponent who succeeds.

Be the last to criticize a colleague who fails.

Be sure where your next step will fall, so that you will not stumble.

Be sure of your final destination, in case you are going the wrong way.

Be loving to those who love you.

Some athletes succeed because they are destined to, but most athletes succeed because they are determined to.

Associate yourself with those of good quality if you esteem your own reputation: for it is better to be along than in bad company.

–George Washington

Pass protection is a team proposition, and you must care about each other to the extent that you will sacrifice your own body to help a fellow lineman and protect your quarterback.

The totally dedicated and committed will hustle all the way and make the game breaker. You must have it to win.

How an individual *plays* the game shows something of his or her character. How he or she *loses* shows all of it.

You Tell on Yourself

You tell what you are by the friends you seek,
By the very manner in which you speak
By the way you employ your leisure time,
By the use you make of the dollar and dime.

You tell what you are by the things you wear,
By the spirit in which your burdens you bear,
By the kinds of things at which you laugh,
By the records you play on your phonograph.

You tell what you are by the way you walk,
By the things of which you delight to talk,
By the manner in which you bear defeat,
By so simple a thing as how you eat.

By the books you choose from the well-filled shelf,
In these ways and more, you tell on yourself,
So there's really no particular sense
In any effort at false pretense.

Quality is never an accident; it is always the result of high intention, sincere effort, intelligent direction, and skillful execution; it represents the wise choice of many alternatives.

You wouldn't worry about what people think of you if you could know how seldom they do.

To me, character is being able to say 'yes' and 'no' to the right and wrong things.
—Bill McCartney

The individual who has developed an integrated personality finds it easier to be consistent in his thinking and actions, irrespective of the tension of the situation. Competitive sports offer rich opportunities for the development of the unified personality in that the individual has numerous opportunities to lead and to follow, to give and to take, to submerge self for the good of the common cause, to win, to lose, and take the consequences of your actions and those of the group. In one of his public utterances, Theodore Roosevelt once observed that it was not the critic who counted, nor the one who pointed out how the strong man stumbled or where they could have done a better job. Rather, the credit belongs to the competitor, who strives valiantly, errs often, and frequently comes short, but who is fired with great enthusiasm and great devotion which prompts him to spend himself in a worthy cause. If the competitor fails, he does so while daring greatly, thus evaluating himself to a higher plane than that of the cold and timid soul who has experienced neither victory nor defeat.

Where we go and what we do advertises what we are.

The vision that you glorify in your mind, the ideal that you enthrone in your heart; by this you will build your life. This you will become. Thought and character are one. Good thoughts bear good fruit. The higher a man lifts his thoughts, the greater his achievement. Cherish your dreams and ideals. Keep your goal forever in your mind, for as a man thinketh, so he is.

How Did You Die?

Did you tackle that trouble that came your way with a resolute heart and cheerful? Or hide your face from the light of day with a craven soul and fearful? Oh, a trouble's a ton, or a trouble's an ounce, or a trouble is what you make it, and it isn't the fact that you're hurt that counts, but only how did you take it?

You are beaten to earth? Well, well, what's that! Come up with a smiling face. It's nothing against you to fall down flat, but to lie there, that's disgrace. The harder you're thrown, why the higher you bounce: Be proud of your blackened eye! It isn't the fact that you're licked that counts: It's how did you fight, and why?

And though you be done to the death, what then? If you battled the best you could: If you played your part in the world of men, why, the critic will call it good. Death comes with a crawl, or comes with a pounce, and whether he's slow or spry, it isn't the fact that you're dead that counts, but only how did you die?

–Edmund Vance Cooke

Discipline

Discipline is the basis of true democracy, for it means the adherence of the individual to the set of rules which humankind, through the experience of the ages, has found best suited to govern the relations between the individual members of society so as to protect the interests of the whole. Some of these rules are made by duly constituted authority and laid down in writing. These are called laws. Others have their sanction in custom and usage, and are called conventions. Everyone is always subject to some sort of discipline. Even the Neanderthal or the wild animal must observe the discipline imposed by nature; while the civilized human must observe that imposed the home, the school, the church, the office, the hotel, the street car, the traffic cop, or even the traffic light on the corner.

The decent citizen and the happy one is the one who accepts the discipline cheerfully or else flees from the structures of community living.

Discipline implies subjection to a control exerted for the good of the whole, the adherence to rules or policies extended for the orderly coordination of effort. The employees of every business establishment must conform to the orders and rules of conduct considered necessary by its management, or the business perishes.

Thomas Jefferson's Philosophy

In matters of principle, stand like a rock, in matters of taste, swim with the current. Give up money, give up fame, give up science, give the earth itself and all it contains, rather than do an immoral act. Never suppose that, in any possible situation or under any circumstance, it is best for you to do a dishonorable thing, though it can never be known but to you. Whenever you are to do a thing, though it can never be known but to yourself, ask yourself how you would act were all the world looking at you, and act accordingly.

They who permit themselves to tell a lie once, find it much easier to do it a second and third time, 'til at length it becomes habitual. They tell a lie without attending to it, and truths without the world's believing them.

Intelligence plus character—this is the goal of true education.

—Martin Luther King

Do not speak evil of one another, brethren.

—James 4:11

The trouble with most of us is that we would rather be ruined by praise than saved by criticism.

If any little word of mine may make a life the brighter, if any little song of mine may make a heart the lighter, God help me to speak the little word and take my bit of singing and drop it in some lonely vale, to set the echoes ringing.

—Anonymous

Whatever Happened to "Yes, Please"?

From United Technologies

It went the way of "Thank you," "Excuse me," Yes, sir." Do you know who just about killed all those phrases? All of us. We did not use them enough. We now get "Huh?" "What?" "Gimme more." Mannerly responses are learned at home. Rude, barbaric responses also are learned at home. William of Wykeham, who was born in 1324, said, "Manners maketh man." If we're so smart in the 20th century, how come we're not as civilized as William was in the 14th century? To the child who says, "Huh?" pass along this page.

Myself

I have to live with myself and so I want to be fit for myself to know
I want to be able, as days go by,
Always to look myself straight in the eye;
I don't want to stand, with the setting sun,
And hate myself for things I have done.

I don't want to keep on a closet shelf
A lot of secrets about myself,
And fool myself, as I come and go,
Into thinking that nobody else will know
The kind of man I really am;
I don't want to dress up myself in sham.
I want to go out with my head erect,
I want to deserve all men's respect;
But here in the struggle for fame and pelf
I want to be able to like myself.
I don't want to look at myself and know
That I'm bluster and bluff, an empty show.

I can never hide myself from me;
I see what others may never see,
I know what others may never know,
I never can fool myself, and so,
Whatever happens, I want to be
Self-respecting and with conscience free.

–Edgar A. Guest

Keep Your Patience...

For if you lose it, you lose your composure, confidence, assurance, will, and success.

Patience is victorious:
Oftentimes outruns skill and outwits impulsiveness. Patience is productive: in time the mulberry leaf becomes silk.

Patience is visionary:
Visualizes the ripened grain as the fruition of a series of successive steps of working and waiting—securing the land, breaking the soil, and planting the seed. Nature is wise enough to wait and persistent enough to eventually have her way; and so we can, if we will add patience to diligence.

Patience is a possessor:
The world belongs to those who bide their time.

—Leroy Brownlow

It's Simply Great...

It is great to be alive, and be a part of all that's going on; to live and work and feel and see life lived each day from early dawn; to rise, and with the morning light, go forth until the hours grow late, then joyously return at night and rest from honest toil—it's great. It is great to be a living part of all the surging world alive, and lend a hand in field and mart, a worker in his human hive; to live and earn and dare to do, nor ever shirk or deviate from course or purpose we pursue until the goal is won—it's great!

Self-discipline is a must. A man who loses his temper and uses illegal tactics hurts our team and has no place playing football.

The best things in life are free—it's the worst things that are so expensive.

Integrity

It cannot be bought and it cannot be measured in money. It is a prerequisite in determining the fiber and character of an individual and an organization. Integrity demands that there be no twilight zone—something is either right or it is wrong; black or it is white. Principles may be inborn ethics or, sometimes, mandated. But integrity requires scourging moral courage, magnetized by a fervor for an ideal. The complete person is a union of unswerving integrity, pulsating energy, and rugged determination—and the greatest of these is integrity. One individual with integrity is a majority.

To reflect integrity is to invite trust. To possess integrity is to command respect. Integrity is found in simple issues and those complex. Its presence is critical. It demands total loyalty, a commitment to cause, a dedication to mission, an unflagging determination. Morals, Ethics, Standards, and Integrity, from these flow a torrent of values. Deeds, not words. It is clear that what you do and what you are speak with deafening impact, not what you say you are. Honesty isn't the best policy. It is the only policy: for an individual and an organization, integrity isn't a sometimes thing. It is everything.

If

If you can trust yourself though others doubt you and conquer fears that limit what you dare, so you can freely give to those about the skills and talents that are yours to share:

If you can live not for your pleasure only, but gladly lend your gentleness and grace to warm the hearts of those whose lives are lonely and help to make their world a better place…

If you can be courageous when defeated and humble in the face of victory, or give your best until a task's completed, however difficult that task may be:

If you can strive, not caring who gets credit, and work at building bridges and not walls, or, hearing idle slander, just forget it and never fail to help someone who falls:

If you can take resources that surround you and use them in the way you feel you should, you'll be an adult…and all those around you will be the richer for your maturity!

They enjoy much who are thankful for much; a grateful mind is both a great and happy mind.

The Art of Maturity

The distilled experience of many individuals reveal these discoveries about the art of mature living…

That life is too short to be wasted in hatred, revenge, fault-finding, prejudice, intolerance, and destruction.

That only the affirmative approach inspires progress. We should follow the advice of Charles W. Eliot and "cultivate a calm nature, expectant of good."

That our basic direction should always be toward wholeness of life. The great life is built on deep and enduring values. Like a giant tree, we should grow from within.

That no outstanding work is done alone. Miracles can be achieved when we don't care who gets the credit.

That we should not dodge reality or turn our backs on situations that must be faced. Private bravery is the price of personal victory.

That moderation in all things is a good rule. It is wise to live a balanced and varied life without permitting anyone or anything to enslave us.

That time is the great healer of hurts, sorrows, and disappointments. When one door closes another will open if we don't lose heart.

–Wilferd Peterson

Reputation is what others say about you on your tombstone, character is what angels say about you before the throne of God.

–William Davis

Followers will never go any farther than their leaders.

Why Coaches Are Liked

According to a survey made by the Ohio Football Coaches Association, the coaches kids really like are:

First is the supporter. The type of coach that is at the athlete's side when emotional support is most needed. He or she understands mistakes and offers encouragement for future performances. Kids want to be corrected when they make a mistake.

The second type of coach the players like is "Mr. Cool." Coaches that can handle pressure situations. He or she is the positive model of self-control who knows how to settle the athletes down.

Third, the players like the coach that is referred to as the "shrink," the type that can get them "up" for certain games; a coach that knows something about them and understands that players have bad days and good days; coaches that are perceptive and can help kids that are having problems.

Why Coaches Are Disliked

First is the insulter. He or she is the most disliked type of coach. Every time a kid says something the coach "puts him or her down" and makes the kid feel very small.

Second is the shouting coach. He or she thinks success is dependent on the "decibel rating." The kid drops the ball and the coach shouts out. "You dropped the ball." The loud-mouth coach yells at the kids because he or she thinks it makes him or her a better coach.

Third is the negative coach or the avenger. Everything the kid does the coach says, "What are you trying to do, get me to lose my job?"

Fourth is the choker. They are great practice coaches, but when the game comes around they "choke" under the pressure.

I know it sounds selfish, wanting to do something no one else has done, but that's what you're out here for—to separate yourself from everyone else.

–Jack Nicklaus

The best coach is the coach that treats every player as he would want his own son or daughter to be treated.

Ten Commandments of a Good Sport

A famous sportswriter once compiled what he called the "Ten Commandments" of a good sport. At the same time, he pointed out they can also apply to any and every sort of contest in which human beings take part.

Thou shalt not quit.

Thou shalt not alibi.

Thou shalt not gloat over winning.

Thou shalt not sulk over losing.

Thou shalt not take unfair advantage.

Thou shalt not ask odds thou art unwilling to give.

Thou shalt always be willing to give thine opponent the advantage of the shade.

Thou shalt not underestimate an opponent, or overestimate thyself.

Remember that the game is the thing, and they who think otherwise are not true athletes.

Honor the game thou playeth, for they who playeth the game straight and hard win, even when they lose.

Although these Ten Commandments were written previous to 1942, they still hold many truths and can enable us to be good sports.

You can't control the length of your life, but you can control its width and depth.

You can't control the contour of your countenance, but you can control its expression.

You can't control the other fellow's opportunities, but you can grasp your own.

You can't control the weather, but you can control the moral atmosphere that surrounds you.

You can't control hard times or rainy days, but you can bank money now to boost you through both.

Why worry about things you can't control?

Get busy controlling things that depend on you.

3

Courage

❖

Leadership

Courage—A mental quality, which recognizes fear of danger or criticism but enables the individual to meet danger or opposition with calmness and firmness.

Leadership—The art of influencing and directing others in such a way as to obtain their willing obedience, confidence, respect, and loyal cooperation in order to accomplish the mission.

Photo: Craig Jones/Getty Images

My Creed

I do not choose to be common. It is my right to be uncommon…if I can. I seek opportunity—not security. I do not wish to be a kept citizen, humbled and dulled by having the State look after me. I want to take the calculated risk; to dream and to build, to fail and to succeed. I refuse to barter incentive for a dole. I prefer the challenges of life to the guaranteed existence, the thrill of fulfillment to the stale calm of Utopia. I will not trade freedom for beneficence, nor my dignity for a handout. I will never cower before any master or bend to any threat. It is my heritage to stand erect, proud, and unafraid; to think and act for myself, enjoy the benefits of my creations, to face the world boldly and say: *"This is what I have done."*

—Dean Alfan

Courage is what it takes to stand up and speak.
Courage is also what it takes to sit down and listen.

Conservative coaches have one thing in common: they are unemployed.

—Chuck Knox

You can't be common. The common goes nowhere. You must be uncommon to be champion.

A leader is best when people barely know she exists…when her work is done, her aim fulfilled, they will say, "We did this ourselves."

Courage consists not in blindly overlooking danger, but in seeing it and conquering.

It's been said football is a contact sport. Not so! Football is a collision sport: Dancing is a contact sport.

–Duffy Daugherty

A good team leader is someone who takes a little more than her share of the blame and a little less than her share of the credit.

Don't be afraid to take a big step if one is indicated. You can't cross a chasm in two small jumps.

Leaders have two important characteristics: first they are going somewhere; second they are able to persuade other people to go with them…

There Are a Few Left

Who put the game above the score,
Who rate the battle as the test,
Who stand content, amid the roar,
Where they have given out their best;
No matter what the prize at stake,
Who prove that they can give—and take.

Who have no fear of some defeat,
No vain regrets to haunt their night,
Because the race went to the fleet,
Because the stronger won the fight;
Who do their stuff—win, lose, or draw,
And laugh at fate's inconstant law.

–Grantland Rice

The Responsibilities of Sportsmanship

The Player...

- Treats opponents with respect.
- Plays hard, but plays within the rules.
- Exercises self-control at all times, setting the example for others to follow.
- Respects officials and accepts their decisions without gesture or argument.
- Wins without boasting, loses without excuses, and never quits.
- Always remembers that it is a privilege to represent the school and community.

The Coach...

- Treats own players, and opponents, with respect.
- Inspires in the athletes a love for the game and the desire to compete fairly.
- Is the type of person he/she wants the athletes to be.
- Disciplines those on the team who display un-sportsmanlike behavior.
- Respects the judgment and interpretation of the rules by the officials.
- Knows he/she is a teacher, and understands the athletic arena is a classroom.

The Official...

- Knows the rules.
- Places welfare of the participants above all other considerations.
- Treats players and coaches courteously and demands the same from them.
- Works cooperatively with fellow officials, timers, and/or scorers for an efficient contest.
- Is fair and firm in all decisions, never compensating for a previous mistake.
- Maintains confidence, poise, and self-control from start to finish.

The Spectator...

- Attempts to understand and be informed of the playing rules.
- Appreciates a good play no matter who makes it.
- Cooperates with and responds enthusiastically to cheerleaders.
- Shows compassion for an injured player; applauds positive performances; does not heckle, jeer, or distract players; and avoids use of profane and obnoxious language and behavior.
- Respects the judgment and strategy of the coach, and does not criticize players or coaches for loss of a game.
- Respects property of others and authority of those who administer the competition.
- Censures those whose behavior is unbecoming.

Paradoxical Commandments of Leadership

1. People are illogical, unreasonable, and self-centered. Love them anyway.

2. If you do good, people will accuse you of selfish ulterior motives. Do good anyway.

3. If you are successful, you win false friends and true enemies. Succeed anyway.

4. The good you do today will be forgotten tomorrow. Do good anyway.

5. Honesty and frankness make you vulnerable. Be honest and frank anyway.

6. The biggest people with the biggest ideas can be shot down by the smallest people with the smallest ideas. Think big anyway.

7. People favor underdogs but follow only top dogs. Fight for a few underdogs anyway.

8. What you spend years building may be destroyed overnight. Build anyway.

9. People really need help but may attack you if you help them. Help them anyway.

10. Give the world the best you have and you'll get kicked in the teeth. Give the world the best you have anyway.

Only the small at heart are ashamed of doing small things and filling small assignments. The truly secure, self-confident person has no fears and shares a trait with history's greatest leaders—humility.

When you ask someone to do a job, first be sure in your mind what it is you want.

Good leaders were first great followers.

Fatigue makes cowards of us all...

–Vince Lombardi

Have ideals and live with them…

You have to have courage to make a decision and stick with it knowing that people are going to criticize you no matter what you do.

No one can make you feel inferior without your consent.

Common sense is really not all that common.

Courage is fear that has said its prayers…

Fat cats don't fight…

Upsets don't just happen. They are planned.

Everything is easier said than done.

Keep your fears to yourself, but share your courage with others.

Believe in yourself.

The football coach has a lonely job, he rarely gets much credit. And if he hears a kindly word…this is the group that said it.

He labors hard to build the sport, in a manner almost stately. But the only question he's ever asked is: "What have you won for us lately?"

And so you coaches, hear my wish, and don't sink into lethargy. Have some fun—there are a lot worse things than being burned in effigy!

–President Ford to NFCA, 1975

When success turns an athlete's head, she faces failure.

About all there is to success is making promises and keeping them…

There is no scrap in scrapbooks.

Courage is the first of human qualities because it is the quality which guarantees all others.

–W. Churchill

Mud thrown is ground lost.

Good leaders learn to share decisions with others even though they alone must accept responsibility for the results.

Leadership usually begins with a vision of success; a glimmering intuition that solutions to problems are possible.

What Today Will Bring

This is the beginning of a new day. God has given me this day to use as I will. I can waste it or use it for good. What I do today is important, because I'm exchanging a day of my life for it.

When tomorrow comes this day will be gone forever, leaving in its place something I have traded for it.

I want it to be gain, not loss; good, not evil; success, not failure.

In order that I shall not regret the price I paid for it because the future is just a whole string of nows.

A person who cannot lead and will not follow invariably obstructs.

"Fight on, my men," Sir Andrew says, "A little I'me hurt, but yett not slaine; I'le but lye down and bleede awhile, and then I'll rise and fight againe."

Nobody said life would be easy…and you only make it tougher if you feel sorry for yourself.

—Morley Fraser

Courage conquers all things.

The Only Way To Win

It takes a little courage, and a little self-control
And some grim determination, if you want to reach your goal.
It takes some real striving, and a firm and stern-set chin,
No matter what the battle, if you really want to win.
There's no easy path to glory, there's no rosy road to fame,
Life, however, we may view it, is no simple parlor game.
But its prizes call for fighting, for endurance and for grit,
For a rugged disposition and a "don't-know-when-to-quit."
You must take a blow or give one, you must risk and you must lose;
And expect that in the struggle you will suffer from the bruise.
But you must not wince or falter, if a fight you once begin;
Be a man and face the battle—that's the only way to win.

One individual plus courage is a majority.

Leaders first supply light then they apply the heat!

I tell my people you treat me fair, I'll treat you fair. You tell me the truth. I'll tell you the truth. You may hate my guts because you believe something I don't but we'll both know where we stand.

—Bo Schembechler

They that lose money lose little.
They that lose health lose much.
But they that lose courage lose all.

It's not the size of the dog in the fight. It's the size of the fight in the dog.

Leadership

Leaders understand and appreciate people.

Their interest is shown through kindness, courtesy, fairness, and unlimited patience.

They know the people in their organization and treat those in minor and major positions with equal consideration.

They have great capacity for work but do not try to do it all themselves. They delegate authority and responsibility. They have unbounded enthusiasm for their organization, its product, their associates, their profession, and their country.

As Knute Rockne put it:
"When the going gets tough, the tough get going."

The art of courage is the realization that no problem is insurmountable if you have confidence in yourself and in the Supreme Source of all courage.

Courage is the antidote for fear…man's greatest enemy. The art of courage is filling our minds with courageous thoughts and overcoming ourselves to conquer life's obstacles.

Courage is quaking knees and a quivering heart, and the faith, perseverance, determination, and daring to carry on in spite of them.

Courage is ACCOMPLISHMENT.

There is a thin line between discipline and harassment.
Discipline breeds success, harassment breeds contempt.

Happy are those who dream dreams and are ready to pay the price to make them come true.

Would you be willing to preach what you practice?

To know what is right and not do it is a definition of a coward.

The Art of Courage

The art of courage makes mountaintop individuals out of ordinary individuals. It is an essential ingredient in those of outstanding accomplishment.

In the words of Sydney Smith, "A great deal of talent is lost for want of a little courage."

The art of courage causes some to keep on trying where others have failed, and, in rising above failure, to invent the light bulb, the airplane, and the penicilins.

"Courage is the human virtue that counts most," wrote Robert Frost. It makes people venture into the unknown. It stretches their horizons. It enlarges their visions. It magnifies their capabilities.

Courage is the acceptance of what and where we are and living abundantly in spite of it.

The greatest test of courage on earth is to bear defeat without losing heart.

Those of courage rise to a challenge, dare to try the untried, and carry on in spite of defeat because they know it is only a temporary setback.

Those of courage take over where others stop and go on to win the important battles in war, science, politics, business, and all of life.

If our game is to be a preparation for life, then it must be more than relaxing play. Caesar put it well when he said: "Cowards die many times before their deaths, the valiant never taste of death but once." Courage is one of the things our game teaches. The way to drain the life out of sport is to take it lightly. I hope my players also learn that neither winning not losing is as important as what they learn about themselves.

Leadership

The road to leadership is danger-laden. No easy task, this. Leaders must be willing to take the risk, the blame, the brunt, and the storm. Never the easy way. Never safety first. There is a zeal for adventure. A willingness to endure. A devotion to work. A passion to win.

Leaders have low tolerance for idleness. No regular office hours for them. They recognize that to stay on top is more difficult than the journey to get there. They do not understand the forty-hour week. What they seek is the forty-hour day. There is a sacrificial willingness to pay the price. Laboriously, painstakingly, they extend new frontiers. There is a driving, ceaseless commitment to the task. An indomitable persistence. An immense sustained urge to succeed. They thrive on the discipline and struggle of adversity.

An uncommon individual, the leader. He or she is a nonconformist, a dissenter, a malcontent, and will do anything to escape the tyranny of mediocrity. They understand that the difference between failure and success is often the difference in doing something nearly right and doing it exactly right. They have the power to persuade and inspire others to heights they thought unreachable.

They are energy and enthusiasm in motion. Willing to try anything once. They know that no great plan is ever achieved without meeting obstacles others thought impossible.

Progress comes from the intelligent use of experience.

Freedom is nothing but a chance to be better.

–Albert Camus

The one who follows a crowd will never be followed by a crowd.

In every field of human endeavor, those that are first must perpetually live in the white light of publicity. Whether the leadership be vested in a person or in a manufactured product, emulation and envy are ever at work. In art, in literature, in music, in industry, in athletics, the reward and the punishment are always the same. The reward is widespread recognition, the punishment, fierce denial and detraction.

When a person's work becomes a standard for the whole world, it also becomes a target for the shafts of the envious few. If the work were merely mediocre, he or she will be left severely alone. If he or she achieves a masterpiece, it will set a million tongues a-wagging. Jealousy does not protrude its forked tongue at the artist who produces a commonplace painting.

Leaders are assailed because they are leaders, and the effort to equal them is merely added proof of that leadership. The follower seeks to depreciate and to destroy. There is nothing new in this, and it all avails nothing.

If the leader truly leads, he or she remains the leader, master poet, master painter, master coach, master workman. That which is good or great makes itself known. That which deserves to live, lives.

Truth is such a valuable possession that you have to watch it very carefully.

Living with Criticism

Our size is determined by the size of the thing it takes to get our goat.

Criticism upsets the mind that is greedy for praise. If we are quite sure we have done nothing to deserve a reproach, we may treat it with contempt and be safe in so doing.

True appreciation of our own value will make us indifferent to insult.

The art of being wise is the art of knowing what to overlook.

Criticism is an accelerator button on the switch that controls the race of Life. It is a signal to stop running and start flying.

It is all in vain to preach of the truth,
To the eager ears of trusting youth,
If, whenever youth is standing by,
They see you cheat and they hear you lie.
Fine words may grace the advice you give,
But youth will learn from the way you live.

Honor's a word that a coach may use,
High-sounding language the base may choose.
Speech is empty and preaching vain,
Though the truth shines clear and the lesson's plain:
If you play false he will turn away,
For your life must square with the things you say.

He won't tread the path of your righteous talk,
But will follow the path, which you daily walk.
"Not as I do, but do as I say,"
Won't win him to follow the better way.
Through the thin veneer of your speech he'll see
Unless you're the person you would have him be.

The longer you live you will find this true:
As you would teach, you must also do.
If you'd teach him to live to his very best
You must live your life by the self-same test.

Never put your finger on someone's faults unless it's part of a helping hand.

Leadership is action, not position.

–Donald McGannon

Teams are more easily led than driven.

The Coach in Retrospect at the End of the Day

If you sit down at set of sun and count the acts that you have done and counting, find one self-denying deed, one word that eased the heart of him who heard—one glance most kind that fell like sunshine where it went, then you may count that day well spent.

But if, through all the live-long day, you've cheered no heart; if, through all you've done that you can trace, that brought the sunshine to one face—no act most small that helped some soul and nothing cost, then count that day as worse than lost.

—George Eliot

It is not the critic who counts, nor the person who points out how the strong one stumbled, or where the doer of deeds could have done them better.

Upon the fields of friendly strife are sown the seed that, upon other fields, on other days, will bear the fruits of victory.

—Gen. Douglas MacArthur

We are all alike; we have eyes, ears, arms, legs, and a head. The difference is in the heart.

The Samurai of Japan used to say: "Remove your ego from the battle and fight the battle for the sake of the battle." Another part of the Samurai creed was: "Do your best, and cast your fate to heaven."

If the blind lead the blind, both shall fall into the ditch.

—Matthew 15:14

These Are My Dreams

My dreams are not tomorrow—nor yesterday. For yesterday is gone, and on its way. And by tomorrow it may be much too late to find my way through darkness and through fate.

When you have reached a certain span in life, today is all that counts, for fun or strife. The past is blurred with fogs and mists and myth. The future is too brief to bother with.

I dream today with no vain, vague regrets for yesterday and all its unpaid debts, with no fear of the future's fading sun, since it may end before this rhyme is done.

I dream of romance and a song that rings above the duller, elemental things, not caring what may happen to skies dark or blue, if I can know that just one dream comes true.
                                                              –Grantland Rice.

It is frequently a misfortune to have very brilliant men in charge of affairs. They expect too much of ordinary men.

                                                              –Thucydides

The question "Who ought to be boss?" is like asking, "Who ought to be the tenor in the quartet?" Obviously, the one who can sing tenor.

                                                              –Henry Ford

It is hard to look up to a leader who keeps his ear to the ground

                                                              –James H. Boren

Courage is not the absence of fear, but the mastery of it.

                                                              –Mark Twain

The Courage to Dare

The course of history has been changed by those willing to dare, and those daring enough to do. Life is an exciting adventure, but is also a struggle. Every great success has been achieved by those who are willing to dare, and every winner has scars.

Courage requires ambition, integrity, audacity, and the will to succeed.

Courage requires a drive to be different. It is escaping from old ideas and patterns and breaking the barriers of accepted ways of doing things. A systematic pursuit to plunge, to speculate, to inquire, to imagine, to doubt, to explore.

Courage requires a healthy impatience, unencumbered by standard procedures and un-dissipated by the bonds of custom and restraint. Eccentric experimentation and radical departure are the rule. The one who dares is willing to forge the unknown and place new ideas in confrontation with the old. It is a venturous gospel, the courage to dare. It takes a spirit that welcomes non-conformity, filled with zeal, exuberance, and an ardor for the unexplored. And the travel is worthy of the travail.

Failure is not final or fatal, but not to make the attempt is the great failure. The one with courage is unafraid of making mistakes. He or she is willing to take the calculated risk and act on the belief in his or her own ideas.

Courage comes with great effort, labor, and self-sacrifice.

There must be a willingness to pay the price, and the price is always pain and work along with an uncritical and unquestioning faith.

Courage takes the will, the fortitude, and the resolution of undisciplined enthusiasm. It develops from within and is rooted in a strong mental and moral fiber. It toughens the spirit and strips the fat of indecision. It requires the strength to endure the burden and rigors of the unknown and the heart to expand new horizons and extend new frontiers.

The courage to dare requires abhorrence for everything that is dull, motionless and un-risking. There must be no tolerance for the rigidity and the timidity of attempting the bold and the new. History will deal kindly with the person who throws himself into battle, takes the unconventional position, and gives his heart and spirit to the terror, the surprise, the fear, and the exhilaration of the unexplored. The courage to dare is both the genius and the secret of the ages.

A Prayer Found in Chester Cathedral

Give me good digestion, Lord,
And also something to digest;
Give me a healthy body, Lord,
With sense to keep it at its best.

Give me a healthy mind, good Lord,
To keep the good and pure in sight;
Which, seeing sin, is not appalled,
But finds a way to set it right.

Give me a mind that is not bored,
That does not whimper or sigh;
Don't let me worry overmuch
About the fussy thing called "I."

Give me a sense of humor, Lord
Give me the grace to see a joke;
To get some happiness from life,
And pass it on to other folk.

Dykes of Courage

Courage and cowardice are antithetical.

Courage is an inner resolution to go forward in spite of obstacles and frightening situations; cowardice is a submissive surrender to circumstance.

Courage breeds creative self-affirmation; cowardice produces destructive self-abnegation.

Courage faces fear and thereby masters it; cowardice represses fear and is thereby mastered by it.

Courageous men never lose the zest for living even though their life situation is restless; cowardly men, overwhelmed by the uncertainties of life, lose the will to live.

We must constantly build dykes of courage to hold back the flood of fear.

–Martin Luther King

Style

When you have it, all else is easy. An organization with style, like a person with style, stands out. An indescribable élan. The world takes note.

Style has no fixed laws, no easily definable shape. It is as elusive as a moonbeam. It is the essence of character, yet with no recognizable features all its own. Style is an elusive quality, wholly dependent on the individual or the organization that possesses it. A successful and extraordinary blend of form and content, authenticity and integrity.

When a woman has style she has a singular distinction. A unique flair marks everything she does—an éclat. Her work, her appearance, her whole vibrant being reflects strength, creativity, accomplishment, and most of all confidence.

Sometimes, but not often, an individual seems virtually born with a highly impressed sense of her own style. From childhood, she knows she is destined to be different. She understands that others will turn naturally to her for guidance. She accepts as inevitable that she will lead, create change, tackle the impossible, and win. She etches her goals early, she develops an approach, and she plunges.

But the serious organization must not deliberately set out to create a style of its own. It cannot be done. The harder a group tries, the less likely it is to achieve this gossamer quality. Style that is calculated and forced is not style at all, but a sham. Worse still, gimmickry and mockery. The world is not fooled.

Style is never bought or forced. Style is something magical a person or an organization exudes. Naturally. Its roots are deep and it has an overriding impact on every action. Style cannot be touched, but it can be felt. It is nothing more than an aura, but it is everything.

Energy dispersed in the pursuit of style is energy lost and wasted. But when an organization rivets its focus on priority tasks—on goals, excellence, achievement—then style evolves effortlessly and of its own design and creation.

An organization with style is driven and dedicated by conviction. Obsesses with what would seem to be impossible objectives, it exhilarates in the spotlight. Utterly undaunted, it advanced steadily and determinedly. Style provides the badge of individuality, which separates quality from mediocrity. Style is of unparalleled consequence because it gives witness to an organization's strength, character, and audacity.

You can judge leaders by the size of the problems they tackle—people nearly always pick a problem their own size, and ignore or leave to others the bigger or smaller ones.

–Anthony Jay

Courage is not blindly overlooking danger, but seeing it and conquering it.

–Richter

Repetition may not entertain, but it teaches.

–Bastiat

4

Dedication

❖

Sacrifice

❖

Desire

Some people grin and bear it...
others smile and change it...

Photo: Craig Jones/Getty Images

The one who won't be denied will find a way.

Motivate

Morale—recognize individual—rewards, personal contact—dressing room
Opportunity—getting it—convince with facts—film grade—stats
Togetherness—dressing room unity—pictures—press guide—newspapers
Initiative—encourage to lead—find leaders early
Variety—change off-season program—make practice exciting
Attitude—how do players feel
Tradition—cannot be bought, sold, or bargained for
Energy—teach everyone to start their own engine
It must build…

Pay no attention to what the critics say. A statue has never been erected in honor of a critic.

—Jean Sibelius

If hard work is the key to success, most people would rather pick the lock.

—Claude McDonald

You cannot train a horse with shouts and expect it to obey a whisper.

—Dagabert D. Runes

It is no disgrace to fail, but to lie there and grunt is.

Try and Be the Best

If you can't be the pine on top of the hill,
Be a scrub in the valley—but be
The best little scrub at the side of the hill;
Be a bush if you can't be a tree.

If you can't be a bush, be a but of grass,
Some highway to happier make;
If you can't be a muskie; then just be a bass—
But the liveliest bass in the lake.

We can't all be captains, some have to be crew;
There's something for all of us here;
There's big work to do; there's lesser to do;
And the task we must do is near.

If you can't be a highway, then just be a trail,
If you can't be a sun, be a star.
If isn't by size that you win or you fail—
Be the *best* of whatever you are.

—Joe Dirk

Condition comes from hard work during practice and proper mental and moral conduct between practices.

—John Wooden

I have never heard of anyone stumbling on something big while sitting down.

A fault recognized is half corrected.

Never be satisfied.

Before strongly desiring anything, we should look carefully into the happiness of its owner.
—La Rochefoucauld

You can't hoot with the owls at night and fly with the eagles during the day.

Counting time is not so important as making time count.

Believe in Yourself

Believe in yourself! Believe you were made to do any task without calling for aid.

Believe, without growing too scornfully proud, that you, as the greatest and least are endowed.

A mind to do thinking, two hands and two eyes are all the equipment God gives to the wise.

Believe in yourself! You're divinely designed and perfectly made for the work of mankind.

This truth you must cling to through danger and pain; the heights others have reached you can also attain. Believe to the very last hour, for it's true, that whatever you will, you'be been gifted to do.

Believe in yourself and step out unafraid.

By misgivings and doubt be not easily swayed.

You've the right to succeed; the precision of skill which betokens the great you can earn if you will!

The wisdom of ages is yours if you'll read.

But you've got to believe in yourself to succeed.

Fire your gun, then get ready to fire again, instead of talking about the first shot.

Football is a game that separates the men from the boys. But also, it's a game that makes kids of us all.

–Clettus Atkinson

I'm Gonna Try

I'm gonna try to play the game, and play it hard and play it fair.
I may not always meet the test as well as some more clever "guy,"
But while my heart beats in my chest, I'm gonna try.

I'm gonna try to stand the gaff, yet keep my nerve;
I'm gonna seek to love and work and play and laugh, never show no yellow streak.
I'm gonna struggle to be kind and not grow hard of face and eye.
I'll flop at times, but never mind, I'm gonna try.

I'm gonna try to be a friend that teammates can trust and who they know
Will be the same to the end, whether the luck runs high or low.
I'll hitch my wagon to a star, and set my goal up in the sky.
And though I may not get far, *I'm gonna try*.

Love your enemies; it will drive them crazy.

The word American ends in—I can!

There are three kinds of people in the world…
The wills, the wants, and the can'ts
The first accomplish everything,
The second oppose everything,
The third fail in everything.

There is a big difference between wanting to and willing to.

The Cafeteria

Today I complained about the food in the cafeteria. Forgive me, Lord. Instead of complaining, let me be thankful for the food I ate. There are so many who will die of hunger today in this world. I feel ashamed. Forgive me. Amen.

To achieve all that is possible we must attempt the impossible.

If you can imagine it, you can achieve it.
If you can dream it, you can become it.

The biggest sin in life is wasting time.

Freedom is like a coin. It has the word privilege on one side and responsibility on the other. It does not have privilege on both sides. There are too many today who want everything involved in privilege but many refuse to accept anything that approaches the sense of responsibility.

–Joseph R. Sizoo

Any criticism I make of anyone on my team, I make because they are not performing to their full potential.

–Vince Lombardi

It Can Be Done

Somebody said that it couldn't be done, but with a chuckle replied, that "maybe it couldn't" but he would be one who wouldn't say so till he'd tried. So he buckled right in with the trace of a grin on his face. If he worried, he hid it. He started to sing as he tackled the thing that couldn't be done. And he did it. Somebody scoffed: "Oh, you'll never do that, at least no one has ever done it." So he took off his coat and took off his hat and the first thing he knew he'd begun it. With the lift of his chin and a bit of a grin, if any doubt rose he forbid it. He started to sing as he tackled the thing that couldn't be done, and he did it. There are thousands to point out to you, one by one, the dangers that wait to assail you, but just buckle right in with a bit of a grin, then take off your coat and hat and go to it. Just start to sing as you tackle the thing that cannot be done and you'll do it.

Boosters

I had a little hammer once with which I used to strike
And I went knocking everywhere
At folks I didn't like.

I knocked most everybody
But I found it didn't pay
For when folks saw me coming
They went the other way.

I've thrown away my hammer, now,
As far as I could shoot,
And taken up a booster horn
And you should hear it toot.

I'm glad I'm with the boosters, now,
I like the way they do.
If you'll throw away your hammer,
I'll get a horn for you!

The Never-Say-Die Spirit

The sandlot Midgets
Played the Gas House Bears;
The football was patched and worn,
The field was littered
With tin cans and snares
And clothing was muddy and torn.

Faces were dirty'
The game nearly thru
Shirttails and pant seats were out.
A dozen loose teeth
And a black eye or two
Proved the Midgets had suffered a rout.

The Bears had a score
Of a hundred and two;
The Midgets had yet to score;
The big Midget center
Told his captain, "I'm through
We can't win—I won't play anymore."

The valiant Captain
Strutted his stuff;
Cited cases, by-laws, and tenets;
Says he, "I'll admit that
It looks kinda tough
But an'thing c'n happ'n in two minutes."

Hist'ry sayeth not
How that game came out;
We assume the Gas Houses won it
But if that Captain's in school,
We've no doubt
They've a whale of a team
And he's on it.

—H.V. Porter

There is only one method of meeting life's test:
Just keep on a-striving an' hope for the best.

The important thing is this, to be able at any moment to sacrifice what we are for what we could become.

–Duboise

We must be aggressive for what is right if our way of life is to be saved from those who are aggressive for what is wrong.

Freedom must be constantly won and re-won. It cannot survive unless those who cherish freedom are prepared to nourish, live by, defend, and develop it.

A capable person on earth is more valuable than any precious deposit under the earth.

Everything cometh to those that waiteth, so long as they who waiteth worketh like hell while they waiteth.

Football requires a certain amount of Spartanism. It requires great sacrifice and self denial and you must have control of yourself.

–Vince Lombardi

Success demands singleness of purpose.

One Day at a Time

There are two days in every week about which we should not worry…Two days which should be kept free from fear and apprehension. One of these days is yesterday, with its mistakes and cares, its faults and blunders, its aches and pains. Yesterday has passed forever beyond our control. All the money in the world cannot bring back yesterday. We cannot undo a single act we performed. We cannot erase a single word said. Yesterday s gone!

The other day we should not worry about is tomorrow, with its possible adversities, its burdens, its large promise and poor performance. Tomorrow is beyond our immediate control. Tomorrow's sun will rise, whether in splendor or behind a mask of clouds. But it will rise. Until it does we have no stake in tomorrow, for it is yet unborn.

This leaves only one day…today. Any athlete or coach can fight the battles of just one day. It is when you and I add the burdens of two awful eternities—yesterday and tomorrow—that we break down.

It is not necessarily the experience of today that disturbs one's peace of mind. It is oftentimes the bitterness for something that happened yesterday and the dread of what tomorrow will bring. Let us therefore live one day at a time.

When you hurry in and out of the locker room you hurry in and out of the big leagues.
—Pee Wee Reese

Football is like life—it requires perseverance, self-denial, hard work, sacrifice, dedication, and respect for authority.

—Vince Lombardi

Some of us will do our jobs well and some will not, but we will all be judged by only one thing—the result.

Every game boils down to doing the things you do best, and doing them over and over again.

The amount that can be controlled and executed by a team is controlled by the weakest player on it.

The difference between good and great is just a little extra effort.

–Duffy Daugherty

Food For Thought
Author Unknown

I watched them tearing a building down,
A gang of men in a busy town,
With a ho-heave-ho and a lusty yell
They swung a beam and the sidewall fell.
I asked the foreman: Are these men as skilled
As the men you'd hire if you had to build?
He gave a laugh and said, No indeed
Just common labor is all I need.
I can easily wreck in a day or two
What builders have taken a year to do!
And I thought to myself as I went my way,
Which of these roles have I tried to play?
Am I a builder who works with care,
Measuring life by the rule and square?
Am I shaping my deeds to a well-made plan,
Patiently doing the best I can?
Or am I a wrecker who walks the town
Content with the labor of tearing down?

–Often used by Lou Holtz

Only those who have the patience to do simple things perfectly will acquire the skill to do difficult things easily.

Concentrate on finding your goal, then concentrate on reaching it.
–Col. M. Friedsam

Until one is committed there is hesitancy, the chance to draw back, always ineffectiveness. Concerning all acts of initiative (and creation), there is one elementary truth, the ignorance of which kills countless ideas and splendid plans. That the moment one definitely commits oneself, then providence moves, too. All sorts of things occur to help one that would never otherwise have occurred.
–William H. Murray

Every accomplishment great or small...starts with the decision...I'll try!

he Five "S's" That Are Necessary For Football

1. Spirit
2. Speed
3. Skill
4. Savvy
5. Size

(If you have the first four, don't worry about the fifth.)

No horse gets anywhere till he is harnessed.
No stream ever drives anything until it is confined.
No life ever grows until it is focused, dedicated, and disciplined.

Fall down seven times, get up eight…

Promise Yourself

Promise yourself to be so strong that nothing can disturb your peace of mind. To talk health, happiness, and prosperity to every person you meet. To make all your teammates feel that there is something in them. To look at the sunny side of everything and make your optimism come true. To think only of the best, to work only for the best, and expect only the best. To be just as enthusiastic about the success of others as you are about your own. To forget the mistakes of the past and press on to the greater achievements of the future. To wear a cheerful countenance at all times and give every living creature you meet a smile. To give so much time to the improvement of yourself that you have no time to criticize others. To be too large for worry, too noble for anger, too strong for fear, and too happy to permit the presence of trouble.

–Christian D. Larson

Desire

Desire makes winners in every walk of life.

The degree of success you achieve depends on the amount of sincere desire you have.

The strength of genuine desire makes you go through a problem when other people go around it.

Desire arms you with the courage to say to yourself, "I'm good, but not as good as I ought to be." Lesser people say, "I'm not as bad as a lot of other people."

Desire fosters the sense of job responsibility. Lack of desire is expressed in, "I only work here."

Every great religion, philosophy, invention, or work of art had its creative beginning in the mind of one with Desire.

Desire is the perfect mental antidote for fear, despair, resentment, and jealousy.

Desire is the dynamic motivation behind every worthwhile purpose; it is the inspiration that keeps the flame of progress burning.

If muscles were everything, a bull could catch a rabbit

Never lose sight of your purpose...

During the 1957 World Series, Yankee catcher, Yogi Berra, saw that Hank Aaron had his bat turned the wrong way. Berra says to Hank, "Turn it around so you can see the trademark!" But Hank just kept his eye on the pitcher, saying, "Didn't come up here to read. I came up to hit."

Nothing is too high for a person to reach, but you must climb with care and confidence.

How—When—Where

It is not so much where you live but rather how, why, and when you live that answers in the affirmative (or maybe in the negative) the question—are you fit to live?

It is not so much where you live as how you live, and whether good flows from you through your neighborhood.

And why you live, and whether you aim high and noblest ends pursue, and keep life brimming full and true;

And when you live, and whether time is at its nadir or its prime, and whether you descend or climb.

It is not so much where you live as whether, while you live, to the world you your highest give, and so answer in the positive that you are truly fit to live.

—John Oxenham

Things turn out best for those who make the best of the way things turn out.

Lost wealth may be regained by industry, lost knowledge by study, lost health by temperance; but lost time is gone forever.

What Is a Workout?

A workout is 25% perspiration and 75% determination. Stated another way, it is one part physical exertion and three parts self-discipline. Doing it is easy once you get started.

A workout makes you better today than you were yesterday. It strengthens the body, relaxes the mind, and toughens the spirit. When you workout regularly, your problems diminish and your confidence grows.

A workout is a personal triumph over laziness and procrastination. It is a badge of a winner—the mark of an organized, goal-oriented person who has taken charge of his or her destiny.

A workout is a wise use of time and an investment in excellence. It is a way of preparing for life's challenges and proving to yourself that you have what it takes to do what is necessary. A workout is a key that helps unlock the door to opportunity and success. Hidden within each of us is an extraordinary force. Physical and mental fitness are the triggers that can release it.

A workout is a form of rebirth. When you finish a good workout, you don't simply feel better—you feel better about yourself!

Champions are generally people who try harder, work harder, fail more often, and bounce back more often than most people. Champions expect to do well, work hard to do well, and, above all, refuse to quit.

Every piece of marble has a statue in it waiting to be released by a man of sufficient skill to chip away the unnecessary parts. Just as the sculptor is to the marble, so is the education to the soul. You cannot create a statue by smashing the marble with a hammer, and you cannot by force of arms release the spirit or the soul of man.

—Confucius

A person in her life is what she is already in her thoughts and desires.

A Bag of Tools…

Isn't it strange that princes and kings,
And clowns that caper in sawdust rings,
And common people like you and me,
Are builders for eternity.

Each is given a bag of tools,
A shapeless mass, a book of rules;
And each must make ere life is flown,
A stumbling block or a stepping stone.

–The Old Coach

The Need to Be

To fulfill the need to be who I am in this world is all I ask. I can't pretend to be something I'm not, and I won't wear a mask.

You touched my face with love in your eyes, but will you touch my heart with the understanding that it takes to realize I just can't play a part.

There's the need to be true to myself and make my own mistakes, and not to lean too hard on someone else no matter what it takes.

So if you're sure it's love, just be sure it's love for this thing called me, 'cause I am what I am and I have the need to be.

I'm not fool enough to ever think that I could be the master of my fate, but it's up to me to choose my roads in life; rocky may well be the ones I take.

So, if you're sure it's love, just be sure it's love for this thing called me, 'cause I am what I am, and I have the need to be.

–Jim Weatherly

Positive attitude changes everything.

When nothing seems to help, I go and look at a stonecutter hammering away at his rock perhaps a hundred times without as much as a crack showing in it. Yet, at the hundred and first blow, it will split in two; and I know it was not that blow that did it, but all that had gone before.

—Jacob Riis

Decision

A weary traveler on the highway of life, I came, near the close of the day, to a fork in the road where stood a lad, unable to choose his way.

I saw him gaze at the distant hill where dreams and hopes mount high, then turn to look down the valley road and draw a heartfelt sigh.

"Coach," said he, "will you help me decide which fork of the road to take? The future I know will all depend on the choice of the road I make.

"One road is lonely, rugged, and steep, that leads to heights unknown, and one a pleasant valley road with companions of my own."

I set his feet on the upper road, ere I took the sunset trail. As I turned he waved a hand and I knew he would not fail.

I watched him climb to the summit high, 'til at last he was lost to view. And I breathed a prayer for other lads, confused and uncertain too…

Who walk along the highway of life, 'til they come, at some future day, to a fork in the road, with a choice to make, may it, Lord, be the upper way.

Do not let what you cannot do interfere with what you can do.

Love the thing you do and you will keep doing better and bigger things.

Whenever I have the pleasure of talking with young people around the country I spend a while describing what I call the "3 D's."

Dedication—an enthusiastic willingness to accept, even look forward to, the long hours of practice, conditioning, and preparation necessary for excellence in any type of endeavor.

Desire—Maintaining within a constant ever burning fire to excel. With it you have the stamina, both mental and physical, to put in those long hours.

Discipline—Possessing the inner strength to commit yourself to the rules, regulations, and training needed to achieve excellence and sticking to them.

To me, team success comes before personal glory, and so it should be with you. Thank God for your talents so that you will be humble in victory and gracious in defeat.

Do these things…and you will not only be a better football player, but a well rounded person who is an asset to your team, your community, your country.

—Bart Starr

For Choosing a Calling

Dear Father,

You are the creative origin of all I am and of all I am called to be. With the talents and opportunities I have, how may I serve you best?

Please guide my mind and heart, open me to the needs of my team, my country, and the world, and help me to choose wisely and practically for your honor and glory and for the good of all those whose lives I touch.

Amen.

If

If I had enough "pull"…
If I had money…
If I had a good education,
If I could get a job…
If I had good health…
If I only had time…
If times were better…
If other people understood me…
If conditions around me were only different…
If I could live my life over again…
If I did not fear what "they would say"…
If I had been given a chance…
If other people didn't have it in for me…
If I could only do what I want…
If I had been born rich…
If I could save some money…
If the boss only appreciated me…
If I only had somebody to help me…
If my family understood me…
If I could just get started…
If I had the personality of some people…
If my talents were known…
If everybody did not oppose me…
If people were not so dumb…
If luck were not against me…
If I were sure of myself…
If I were taller…
If I were faster…
If I did not have a past…

If—and this the greatest of them all—if I had the courage to see myself as I really am, I would find out what is wrong with me and correct it. Then, I might have a chance to profit by my mistakes and learn something from the experience of others. For I know that there is something wrong with me, or I would now be where I could have been if I had spent more time analyzing my weaknesses and less time building alibis to cover them.

The Joiner

Jack was out for football,
But he wasn't very good…
He was in too many things,
To practice as he should;
For he was a class officer,
But on the meeting day,
He couldn't spare the time to go
For he was in a play.

The play was coming off next day,
He didn't know his part,
He'd had to miss the practices,
For he was out for art.
The teacher said his poster
Was going to turn out grand
He didn't get it finished though,
For he was in the band.

His trumpet showed great promise,
But on the concert night,
He turned out for boxing,
Got his lip cut in a fight.
He signed up for the bond campaign,
To be the one who sells,
But he couldn't spare the time to work:
He was leading yells.

And Jack was on the yearbook staff,
And his work was always late,
He never met a deadline,
For he was in debate.
So when the prophecy was read,
His class saw him as one
Still so busy being busy
That he never got things done.

–Author Unknown

Nothing splendid has ever been achieved except by those who dared believe that something inside them was superior to circumstance.

Whatever your goal may be, strike out for it. What if you die in the attempt? If you put every shred of yourself into the attempt, you will have had life's one great exhilarating and soul satisfying experience anyhow. When you start out to pursue your dreams, be prepared for a great discovery. It is the effort itself that will give you peace. This peace goes with you as you grow older, becomes your choicest companion, never leaves you. Wrestling this peace from a troubled world is about all there is to the secret of happiness.

–Ralph Waldo Emerson

Ballad of the Game-Fish
"Only the Game-Fish Swims Upstream"

Where the puddle is shallow, the weak fish stay
To drift along with the current's flow;
To take the tide as it moves each day
With the idle ripples that come and go;
With a shrinking fear of the gales that blow
By distant coasts where the Great Ports gleam;
Where the far heights call through the silver glow,
"Only the game-fish swims upstream."

Where the shore is waiting, the minnows play,
Borne by the current's undertow;
Drifting, fluttering on their way,
Bound by a fate that has willed it so;
In the tree-flung shadows they never know
How far they have come from the old, brave dream;
Where the wild gales call from the peaks of snow.

Held with the current the Fates bestow,
The driftwood moves to a sluggish theme,
Nor heeds the call which the Far Isles throw,
"Only the game-fish swims upstream."

–Grantland Rice

I asked of life:
"What have you to offer me?"
And the answer came:
"What have you to give?"

We can do anything we want to do if we stick to it long enough.

–Helen Keller

5

Ambition

Enthusiasm

Some individuals dream of great accomplishments, while others stay awake and do them.

Keep away from people who try to belittle your ambitions. Small people always do that, but the really great make you feel that you, too, can become great.

-Mark Twain

Photo: Jed Jacobsohn/Getty Images

Size isn't everything. The whale is endangered, while the ant continues to do just fine.

Enthusiasm!

That certain something that makes us great—that pulls us out of the mediocre and commonplace—that builds unto us power. It glows and shines—it lights up our faces—Enthusiasm, the keynote that makes us sing and makes others sing with us.

Enthusiasm—the master of friends, the maker of smiles, the producer of confidence. It cries to the world, "I've got what it takes." It tells all that our job is a swell job, that the team we play for just suits us, the goods we have are the best.

Enthusiasm—the inspiration that makes us "wake up and live." It puts spring in our step, a twinkle in our eyes, and gives us confidence in ourselves and our teammates.

Enthusiasm—it changes a deadpan player to a producer, a pessimist to an optimist, a loafer to a go-getter.

Enthusiasm—if we have it, we should thank God for it. If we don't have it, then we should get down on our knees and pray for it.

Upon the plains of hesitation, bleached the bones of countless millions who, on the threshold of victory, sat down to wait, and waiting they died.

Do the very best you can with what you have.

—T. Roosevelt

Enthusiasm without knowledge is like running in the dark.

You are the player who has to decide whether you'll do it or toss it aside. You are the one who makes up your mind whether you'll lead or linger behind. Whether you'll try for the goal that's afar or be contented to stay where you are. Take it or leave it. Here's something to do, just think it over, it's all up to you.

Give the world the best you have
And the best will come back to you.

Some people are confident they could move mountains if only somebody would just clear the foothills out of the way.

You've got to have the goods, my child, if you want to finish strong;
A bluff may work a little while, but not for very long;
A line of talk all by itself will seldom see you through;
You've got to have the goods, my child, and nothing else will do.
The fight is pretty stiff, my child, I'd call it rather tough;
And all along the routes are wrecks of those who tried to bluff;
They could not back their lines of talk to meet the final test,
You've got to have the goods, my child, and that's no idle jest.

Tomorrow Never Comes

Tomorrow comes—then it's today so if you have a debt to pay, or work to finish, don't delay. Tomorrow never comes. It's fatal to procrastinate, until you find it's just too late, and then to put the blame on fate. Tomorrow never comes. The putting right of some mistakes, the gesture that you meant to make, the habit that you vowed to break. Tomorrow never comes. So do it now—for fate can play some funny tricks; time slips away; we cannot see beyond today. Tomorrow never comes.

Enthusiasm in your work is half the battle won.

You will play as you practice.

The right attitude and one arm will beat the wrong attitude and two arms every time.

In and Out

It's IN to care about your job; it's OUT to bite the hand that feeds you.

It's IN to be loyal to the school that pays you; it's OUT to breed discontent.

It's IN to give a little more than expected; it's OUT to split when you haven't finished the task at hand.

It's IN to be courteous—to anticipate the needs of fellow employees and plan accordingly; it's OUT to operate on your own, disregarding your obligation to others.

It's IN to appreciate all the benefits we enjoy; it's OUT to take all the benefits without making the best of what remains.

It's IN to praise fellow workers, while they're alive to hear it; it's OUT to wait until their wakes to say something nice.

It's IN to communicate with each other; it's OUT to withhold what is necessary to operate a school.

It's IN to contribute, to get involved, to remain active; it's OUT to be passive and pessimistic and aloof.

It's IN to work and win; it's OUT to exist and lose.

It's IN to make productive the days that will never come back; it's OUT to let the days drift by and wonder why you died of boredom.

It's IN to love your job; it's OUT to endure it.

—Mary Sweeney

If you don't get everything you want, think of the things you don't get that you don't want.

The Garden of Life

First, plant five rows of P's

> Presence

> Promptness

> Preparation

> Perseverance

> Purity

Next, plant three rows of squash

> Squash gossip

> Squash indifference

> Squash unjust criticism

Then plant five rows of lettuce

> Let us be faithful to duty

> Let us be unselfish and loyal

> Let us obey the rules and regulations

> Let us be true to our obligations and

> Let us love one another

No garden is complete without turnips

> Turn up for meetings

> Turn up with a smile

> Turn up with determination to make everything count for something good and worthwhile.

Even if you're on the right track, you'll get run over if you just sit there.

Ambition is an idol, on whose wing great minds are carried only to extreme; to be sublimely great or to be nothing.

The reason so many people are unhappy today and seeking help to cope with life is that they fail to understand what human existence is all about. Until we recognize that life is not just something to be enjoyed, but rather is a task that each of us is assigned we'll never find meaning in our lives and never truly be happy.

—Dr. Victor Frankl, Holocaust survivor

Neither you nor the world knows what you can do until you have tried.

—Ralph Waldo Emerson

If there's one thing we should let others find out for themselves, it's how great we are.

Some people stay right in the rut while others head the throng.
All individuals may be born equal—but they don't stay that way long.
There is many a person with a gallant air, goes galloping to the fray;
But the valuable one is the one who's there when the smoke has cleared away.
Some say "I don't get nuthin' out of life" but when their whines begin,
We often can remind them that they "Don't put nuthin' in."

We accomplish in proportion to what we attempt.

Three of the most difficult things in life are to keep a secret, forget an injury, and make good use of leisure time.

Commitment to Excellence

I owe everything to football, in which I have spent the greater part of my life. I have never lost my respect, my admiration, or my love for what I consider a great game. Each Sunday, after the battle, one group savors victory; another group lives in the bitterness of defeat. The many hurts seem a small price to have paid for having won, and there is no reason at all that is adequate for having lost. To the winner there is one hundred percent fun; and to the loser the only thing left for him is a one hundred percent resolution, one hundred percent determination.

It's a game, I think, a great deal like life in that it demands that a man's personal commitment be toward victory, even though you know that ultimate victory can never be completely won. Yet it must be pursued with all of one's might. Each week there's a new encounter, each year a new challenge. All of the rings and all of the money and all of the color and all of the display linger only in memory. The spirit, the will to win, and the will to excel, these are the things that endure and these are the qualities that are so much more important than any of the events that occasion them. I would like to say that the quality of any man's life has got to be the measure of that man's personal commitment to excellence and to victory, regardless of what fields he may be in.

–Vince Lombardi

The saddest words of tongue or pen are these sad words… "it might have been."

You only live once—If you do it right, once is enough.

There are few, if any, jobs in which ability alone is sufficient. Needed also are loyalty, sincerity, enthusiasm, and cooperation.

A person who is enthusiastic soon has enthusiastic followers.

Try, Try Again

'Tis a lesson you should heed,
Try, try again;
If at first you don't succeed
Try, try again;
Then your courage should persevere,
You will conquer, never fear;
Try, try again.
Once or twice though you should fail,
Try, try again;
If you would at last prevail,
Try, try again;
If we strive, 'tis no disgrace
Though we do not win each race;
What should you do in this case?
Try, try again.
If you find your task is hard,
Try, try again;
Time will bring you your reward,
Try, try again;
All other folks can do,
Why, with patience, should not you?
Only keep this rule in view,
Try, try again!

–from McGuffey's Reader

If it's worth doing at all, it's worth doing well.

He who would leap high must take a long run.

–Danish Proverb

Do it like it is your last chance.

Whatever you vividly imagine, ardently desire, sincerely believe, and enthusiastically act upon…must inevitably come to pass.

Just for Today

Just for today I will live through the next 12 hours and not tackle my whole life problem at once.

Just for today I will improve my mind. I will learn something useful. I will read something that requires effort, thought, and concentration.

Just for today I will not find fault with a friend, relative, or teammate. I will not try to change or improve anyone but myself.

Just for today I will have a program. I might not follow it exactly, but I will have it. I will save myself from two enemies—hurry and indecision.

Just for today I will exercise my character in three ways. I will do a good turn and keep it a secret.

If anyone finds out, it won't count.

Just for today I will do two things I don't want to do, just for the exercise.

Just for today I will be unafraid. Especially will I be unafraid to enjoy what is beautiful and believe that as I give to the world, the world will give to me.

–Ann Landers, nationally syndicated column, October 1972

Triumph is just umph added to try!

Big shots are usually little shots who kept on shooting.

To activate others, to get them to be enthusiastic, you must first be enthusiastic yourself.

10 Rules for Building Self-Confidence

by Norman Vincent Peale

1. Formulate and stamp indelibly on your mind a mental picture of yourself succeeding.

2. Whenever a negative thought concerning your personal powers comes to mind, deliberately voice a positive thought to cancel it out.

3. Do not build up obstacles in your imagination.

4. Do not be awestruck by other people and try to copy them. Nobody can be you as efficiently as you can.

5. Ten times a day repeat these dynamic words: "If God be for us, who can be against us?"

6. Get a competent counselor to help you understand why you do what you do. Learn the origin of your inferiority and self-doubt feelings, which often begin in childhood. Self-knowledge leads to a cure.

7. Ten times each day practice the following affirmation, repeating it out loud if possible: "I can do all things through Christ, who strengthens me."

8. Make a true estimate of your own ability, then raise it 10 percent.

9. Put yourself in God's hands. To do that simply state, "I am in God's hands."

10. Remind yourself that God is with you and nothing can defeat you.

No one can walk backward into the future.

Good, better, best: Never let it rest, till your good is better, and your better is best.

There is no security in this life, only opportunity.

–Gen. Douglas MacArthur

Our doubts are traitors and make us lose the good we oft might win, by fearing to attempt.

–Shakespeare

People may doubt what you *say*, but they will *always* believe what you *do*.

Momentum

Momentum is everything. It makes all things possible. In an organization, it converts individuals into a team of dedicated devotion. It lifts and transforms them beyond a personal interest and unites them in a common cause.

Momentum requires integrity to say, "We must do better." It is an arduous pledge, because where there is no pain, there is not momentum. It requires the bursting force of energy and indomitable courage. It is the unrelenting quest for breaking the ridig bonds of institutional paralysis. It demands the full effort and commitment of all, galvanized to the highest of ideals. An organization with MOMENTUM has an impelling and infectious urge and surge. A rolling, whirling, booming enthusiasm. An undisciplined fervor for the fray and venture. Forward, always forward. Advancing. Achieving. Always at an accelerating pace.

Momentum doesn't just happen. It requires the electrifying force of a leader. Single-minded and unswerving in the pursuit of an objective, with an ardor and zeal which knows no bounds. It demands an intense, towering energy and a keen sense of destiny and, most of all, the raging vision and passion to be the best.

Momentum is everything…because it drives, directs, and determines the organization's destiny.

Do not take life too seriously. You will never get out of it alive.

Ten Commandments for Handling Ideas

1. I will never vote no to any idea because "it's impossible."

2. I will never block a helpful thought because it entails problems, or wait to begin until I find solutions.

3. I will never oppose a possibility because I've never done it and can't imagine how it could be done.

4. I will never obstruct a plan because it runs a risk of failure.

5. I will never cooperate in defeating a potentially good idea because I can see something wrong with it.

6. I will never squelch a creative idea because no one else has ever succeeded in perfecting it.

7. I will never declare any constructive concept to be impossible because I lack the time, money, brains, energy, talent, or skill to exploit it.

8. I will never discard a plan or project just because it's imperfect.

9. I will never resist a proposal because I didn't think of it, won't get credit for it, won't personally benefit from it, or may not live to see and enjoy it.

10. I will never quit because I've reached the end of the rope, I will tie a knot and hang on!

–Robert H. Schuller

It you aren't going all the way, why go at all?

–Joe Namath

Don't grumble because you don't have what you want.
Be thankful you don't get what you deserve.

Enthusiasm is like a coat of fresh paint.
It covers up a lot of rough spots.

Napoleon once observed, "An army's effectiveness depends on its size, training, experience, and morale…and morale is worth more than all the other factors combined."

Nature has everywhere written her protest against idleness: everything which ceases to struggle or remains inactive rapidly deteriorates. It is the struggle toward an ideal—the constant effort to get higher and further—which develops manhood and character.
—Alfred A. Montapert

Your expression is the most important thing you wear.
—Sid Ascher

Without ambition and enthusiasm for your work the parade will pass you by.

No person who is enthusiastic about work has anything to fear from life.

The biggest trouble with a sure thing is the uncertainty.

If you ask for yourself what you deny others, your asking is a mockery.

The Next Time Around

How many will battle on
When pressure to compromise is strong?
Who is left to make a stand on idealistic ground
And keep the faith the next time around?

The price we pay for standards is severe,
But some must hold out through the price is dear.
The loser is the winner when the inner strength
Is found to fight to his feet the next time around.

To those who are loyal here's my hand.
I will be there when you have to make your stand.
To those who weaken when the chips are down…
I will pray for you the next time around.

It is never safe to look into the future with eyes of fear.

—E. H. Harriman

Did is a word of achievement,

Won't is a word of retreat,

Might is a word of bereavement,

Can't is a word of defeat,

Ought is a word of duty,

Try is a word of each hour,

Will is a word of beauty,

Can is a word of power.

It isn't the thing we do or say, but all in the way we do or say it.
What would the egg amount to, pray, if the hen got up on the perch to lay it?

Endurance

How much the heart may bear and yet not break!
How much the flesh may suffer and not die!
I question if any pain or ache
Of soul or body brings our end more high.
Death chooses its own time: 'til that is sworn
All evil may be borne.

Behold, we live through all things—famine, thirst,
Bereavement, pain, all grief and misery,
All woe and sorrow.
Life inflicts its worst on soul and body,
But we cannot die, though we be sick and tired and faint and worn,
Lo, all things can be borne!

—E. A. Allen

Perk Up

Your nose may be battered, your jaw-bone nicked,
Your visage may be a sight,
But always remember: You're never licked
While still you can stand up and fight.
No matter how badly they mess your map,
It won't be beyond repair,
And there is still a chance that you will
Win the scrap as long as the punch is there.

You'll make mistakes and you'll do things wrong,
The best of them always do,
But as soon as you get to going strong,
Your grit will see you through.
They smashed Paul Jones to a fare-you-well
But he didn't observe "good-night";
He merely paused in his tracks to yell
That he'd just begun to fight.

—James Montague

Too low they build, who build below the sky.

The future always holds something for the individual who keeps faith in it.

The Intended Philosophy of Intercollegiate Athletics

- To nurture and properly channel the competitive urge inherent in all of us and carried with us throughout our lives.
- To engender the will to win, by fair and honest means, in the youth of America.
- To highlight and promote the traditional American pride in successful effort for the sake of accomplishment.
- To build team spirit and a desire on the part of those who engage in sports to work with each other in a cooperative effort.
- To teach self-discipline and self-control.
- To develop morale and mold character in the tradition of American individualism.
- To build sound minds and bodies through mental and physical coordination.
- To encourage spectators and non-participants generally to take an interest in and appreciate the values of competitive effort.
- To stimulate a continuing institutional interest and loyalty among students, alumni, and friends.

Our programs are designed to develop such characteristics as:

- ✓ Loyalty to purpose
- ✓ Respect for discipline, loyalty, and teamwork
- ✓ Capacity to lead and direct
- ✓ Ability to act effectively under stress

No power in the world can keep a first-class person down
or help a fourth-class person up.

The Second Chance

If we might have a second chance to live the days once more, and rectify mistakes we made, to even up the score;

If we might have a second chance to use the knowledge gained, perhaps we might become, at last, as fine as God ordained.

But though we can't retrace our steps, however stands the score,
Tomorrow brings another chance for us to try once more.

Some people get up and go. Others get up and goof.

Undertake something that is difficult; it will do you good. Unless you try to do something beyond what you have already mastered, you will never grow.
–Ronald Osborn

You must have enthusiasm for life, or life is not going to have much enthusiasm for you.

No one is worth his salt who is not ready—at all times—to risk his body, to risk his well-being, and to risk his life for a great cause.

Those willing and able to play—will play!

We rate ability in humans by what they finish, not by what they attempt.

Make Something Happen

You come out of a meeting and someone asks, "What happened?" You answer, "Nothing." In a legislative gallery someone sits down beside you and asks, "What's happening? You say, "Nothing." Maybe that meeting room and that gallery should have had the same sign hanging on their walls that—so the story goes—a particular college football coach pasted in his team's lockers: *Cause Something to Happen*. He believed that if you didn't make something happen with a good block, your runner would go nowhere. If you didn't tackle, the other team would run all over you. He sure caused something to happen. He won more college games than any other coach. His name was Bear Bryant.

The best verse hasn't yet been rhymed
The best house hasn't been planned
The highest peak hasn't yet been climbed
The mightiest rivers aren't spanned
Don't worry and fret, faint-hearted
The chances have just begun
For the best jobs haven't been started
The best work hasn't been done.

May You Have...

Enough HAPPINESS to keep you SWEET
Enough TRIALS to keep you STRONG
Enough SORROW to keep you HUMAN
Enough HOPE to keep you HAPPY
Enough FAILURE to keep you HUMBLE
Enough SUCCESS to keep you EAGER
Enough FRIENDS to give you COMFORT
Enough WEALTH to meet your NEEDS
Enough ENTHUSIASM to look FORWARD
Enough FAITH to banish DEPRESSION
Enough DETERMINATION to make each day better than yesterday.

Let's imitate the good old horse and lead a life that's fitting.
Just pull an honest load, then there'll be no time for kicking.

Ideas

When someone says, "It can't be done," he probably means, "I don't know how to do it." At what exhilarating moment does a new idea spark a barrier-breaking original thought? For Rene Descartes, it came in a stove-heated small room where he lay watching flies on the ceiling over his bed. From his visionary observations of the flies and their changing juxtapositions, Descartes conceived the idea of Geometrical Relationships, which determined the theory of inverted images.

In today's world, to say "impossible" always puts you on the losing side. Every problem is an inspiring opportunity when pursued with a vigorous belief in the possible. A person of ideas is a shaper of "what might be" and not shackled by "what is." An idea is a dream put into action—forceful, determined action.

The wayside is filled with brilliant beings who start with a spurt but lack the stamina and fortitude to finish. Their places are taken by those individuals of ideas who never know when to quit. They have a compelling inner drive, an irrepressible streak to get ahead, and to break their own records. They possess an extraordinary impulse to generate new ideas.

An idea is the mightiest force, the greatest influence on earth. Words and dreams are overabundant, but ideas that rouse can change the world. We touch the highest pinnacle of fulfillment when we are consumed in the quest of an idea.

The coach who has no fire in him surely can't set his team on fire.

The player who is fired with enthusiasm is seldom fired by her coach.

6

Family

Friends

The world needs more warm hearts and fewer hot heads.

An Old Irish Prayer

May those who love us, love us; and those that don't love us, may God turn their hearts; and if He doesn't turn their hearts, may He turn their ankle so we'll know them by their limping.

Photo: Nathan Bilow/Getty Images

From Ann Landers—A father's note to his 17-year-old son and the son's reply years later after his dad's death.

Dear Son: As long as you live under this roof you will follow the rules. In our house we do not have a democracy. I did not campaign to be your father. You did not vote for me. We are father and son by the grace of God. I consider it a privilege and I accept the responsibility. In accepting it, I have an obligation to perform the role of a father.

I am not your pal. The age difference makes such a relationship impossible. We can share many things, but you must remember that I am your father. This is 100 times more meaningful than being a pal.

You will do as I say as long as you live in this house. You are not to disobey me because whatever I ask you to do is motivated by love. This may be hard for you to understand at times, but the rule holds. You will understand perfectly when you have a son of your own.

Until then trust me. Love, Dad.

David apparently had heard a similar message from his own father. He put the clipping in an envelope, with a handwritten note. It read:

Dad: This letter and these feelings have been with me for a long time. It did take having a son to realize how right you were. I now have two sons of my own and I am sounding more like you every day.

I wish we had more time together. I wish I had a chance to tell you how much I've learned.

Thank you for the time we did have.

You taught me well, Dad. I'm just sorry it took me so long. May God bless you.

Love, David

We do not remember days, we remember moments.

Hypocrisy

It is all in vain to preach the truth,
To the eager ears of a trusting youth,
If, whenever the lad is standing by,
He sees you cheat and he hears you lie.
Fine words may grace the advice you give,
But youth will learn from the way you live.
Honor's a word that a thief may use,
High-sounding language the base may choose.
Speech is empty and preaching vain,
Though the truth shines clear and the lesson's plain;
If you play false, he will turn away,
For your life must square with the things you say.
He won't tread the path of your righteous talk,
But will follow the path, which you daily walk.
"Not as I do, but do as I say,"
Won't win him to follow the better way.
Through the thin veneer of your speech he'll see
Unless you're the man you would have him be.
The longer you live you will find this true:
As you would teach, you must also do.
Rounded sentences, smooth and fair,
Were better not said if your deeds aren't square,
If you'd teach him to live to his very best
You must life your life by the self-same test.

—Edgar A. Guest

The best way to better our lot is to do a lot better.

When you help someone up a hill, you'll find yourself close to the top, too.

If good men were only better, would wicked men be so bad?

—J. W. Chadwick

What Are Fathers Made Of?

Paul Harvey, 1992

A father is a thing that is forced to endure childbirth without an anesthetic.

A father is a thing that growls when it feels good—and laughs very loud when it's scared half to death.

A father never feels entirely worthy of the worship in a child's eyes. He's never quite the hero his daughter thinks, never quite the man his son believes him to be—and this worries him, sometimes.

So he works too hard to try and smooth the rough places in the road for those of his own who will follow him.

A father is a thing that gets very angry when the first school grades aren't as good as he thinks they should be. He scolds his son though he knows it's the teacher's fault.

Fathers are what give daughters away to other men who aren't nearly good enough so they can have grandchildren who are smarter than anybody's.

Fathers make bets with insurance companies about who'll live the longest. Though they know the odds, they keep right on betting. And one day they lose.

I don't know where fathers go when they die. But I've an idea that after a good rest, wherever it is, he won't be happy unless there's work to do.

He won't just sit on a cloud and wait for the girl he's loved and the children she bore.

He'll be busy there, too, repairing the stairs, oiling the gates, improving the streets, smoothing the way.

Coming together is a beginning; keeping together is progress; working together is success.

–Henry Ford

What do we live for, if it is not to make life less difficult for each other?

–George Eliot

21 Memos From Your Child

1. Don't spoil me. I know quite well that I ought not to have all I ask for. I'm only testing you.

2. Don't be afraid to be firm with me. I prefer it; it makes me feel more secure.

3. Don't let me form bad habits. I have to rely on you to detect them in the early stages.

4. Don't make me feel smaller than I am. It only makes me behave stupidly "big."

5. Don't correct me in front of others if you can help it. I'll take much more notice if you talk quietly with me in private.

6. Don't make me feel that my mistakes are sins. It upsets my sense of values.

7. Don't protect me from consequences. I need to learn the painful way sometimes.

8. Don't be too upset when I say, "I hate you." It isn't you I hate but your power to thwart me.

9. Don't take too much notice of my small ailments. Sometimes they get me the attention I want.

10. Don't nag. If you do, I shall have to protect myself by appearing deaf.

11. Don't make rash promises. Remember that I feel badly let down when promises are broken.

12. Don't forget that I cannot explain myself as well as I should like. That is why I'm not always very accurate.

13. Don't tax my honesty too much. I am easily frightened into telling lies.

14. Don't be inconsistent. That completely confuses me and makes me lose faith in you.

14. Don't put me off when I ask questions. If you do, you will find that I stop asking and seek my information elsewhere.

16. Don't tell me my fears are silly. They are terribly real and you can do much to reassure me if you try to understand.

17. Don't ever suggest that you are perfect or infallible. It gives me too great a shock when I discover that you are neither.

18. Don't ever think that it is beneath your dignity to apologize to me. An honest apology makes me feel so warm toward you.

19. Don't forget how quickly I am growing up. It must be very difficult for you to keep pace with me, but please try.

20. Don't forget I love experimenting. I couldn't get on without it, so please put up with it.

21. Don't forget that I can't thrive without lots of understanding love, but I don't have to tell you do I?

–The Michigan Elementary Principal, June 1974

It wouldn't be so bad to let one's mind go blank if one always remembered to turn off the sound…

A friend is a present you give yourself.

My Dad

You have been a mighty dandy pal,
You held my baby hand,
You soothed away imagined hurts;
Helped me on my feet to stand.

You always knew each childish want,
And chased away my fears,
Encouraged me when things went wrong,
And wiped away my tears.

Yes, Dad, you walked each day with me.
When the pace was hard and long,
Undying courage you instilled,
Teaching right, condemning wrong.

Your father—wisdom daily gave.
New courage to my heart,
Never tiring, just standing by,
Quietly doing your part.

When now we meet at manhood's gate,
You're the best pal I ever had,
You'll never know what you mean to me,
As I so simply say, "THANKS, DAD!"

—Mamie Oxborn Odum

If you want kids to improve, let them hear the nice things you say about them.

If children live with criticism, they learn to condemn.

If children live with hostility, they learn to fight.

If children live with fears, they learn to be apprehensive.

If children live with pity, they learn to feel sorry for themselves.

If children live with jealousy, they learn to feel guilty.

If children live with encouragement, they learn to be confident.

If children live with tolerance, they learn to be patient.

If children live with praise, they learn to be appreciative.

If children live with acceptance, they learn to love.

If children live with approval, they learn to like themselves.

If children live with recognition, they learn to have a goal.

If children live with fairness, they learn what justice is.

If children live with honesty, they learn what truth is.

If children live with security, they learn to have faith in themselves and in those about them.

If children live with friendliness, they learn that the world is a good place in which to live.

You cannot do a kindness too soon for you never know how soon it will be too late.

A nod, a smile, you scarce believe how much the burden 'twill relieve, thinking the world unfriendly. A gracious work, a kindly deed, does more to help the human need than any doctrine, form or creed. So let's be friendly.

The Ten Commandments of Human Relations

1. Speak to people. There's nothing as nice as a cheerful greeting.

2. Smile at people. It takes 72 muscles to frown and only 14 to smile.

3. Call people by their name. The sweetest music to the ears is one's own name.

4. Be friendly and helpful. If you would have friends, be friendly.

5. Be cordial. Speak and act as if everything you did were a pleasure.

6. Be genuinely interested in people.

7. Be generous with praise, cautious with criticism.

8. Be considerate with the feelings of others; it will be appreciated.

9. Be thoughtful of others' opinions. There are three sides to every controversy—yours, the others—and the right one.

10. Be alert to give service. What counts a great deal in life is what we do for others.

The time to make friends is before you need them.

Be kind. Remember everyone you meet is fighting a hard battle.

It's smart to pick your friends—but not to pieces.

Make new friends but keep the old: the first are silver, the latter gold.

Humans are those foolish creatures who try to get even with their *enemies*—and ahead of their *friends*.

No person stands so tall as when they stoop to help a child.

If I thought that a word of mine perhaps unkind and untrue, would leave its trace on a loved one's face, I'd never speak it—would you?

If I thought that a smile of mine might linger the whole day through and lighten some heart with a heavier part, I'd not withhold it—would you?

True friendship is like sound health, the value of it is seldom known until it is lost.

—C.C. Colton

We're all in this together.

Thank You My Friend

I thank you for the many times you get in touch with me and all your contributions to my happy memory. I thank you for the friendly smile with which you always greet me and for the kind and thoughtful and the gracious way you treat me. You are the shining symbol of a friendship really true; and an inspiration wonderful in all I try to do. You are a soothing comfort to my very smallest sorrow and you instill the hope I need for every new tomorrow. And so I thank you for the joys and favors you extend and pray that God will bless you always my dear and faithful friend.

You can get anything in this world you want if you help enough people get what they want.

Player's Code

- Play the game for the game's sake

- Be generous when you win

- Be graceful when you lose

- Be fair always no matter what the cost

- Obey the laws of the game

- Work for the good of your team

- Accept the decisions of the officials with good grace

- Believe in the honesty of your opponents

- Conduct yourself with honor and dignity

- Honestly and wholeheartedly applaud the efforts of your teammates and your opponents.

The game that this association will support must provide opportunities for:

✓ Fun, enjoyment, and many other recreational satisfactions.

✓ Achievement, recognition, and the pursuit of excellence relative to the skill potential, personal competitive goals, and physio/psycho needs of the participants.

✓ The development of physical, mental, social, and emotional fitness.

The type of game that the association will not support nor tolerate is:

✓ That which brings the game into disrepute.

✓ That which results in physical or mental violence.

✓ That which is morally indefensible.

May the road rise to meet you,
May the wind be always at your back,
May the sun shine warm upon your face,
The rains fall soft upon your fields,
And until we meet again, may God
Hold you in the palm of His hand.

—An Irish Blessing

Parent's Code For Little League

- Children have more need of example than criticism.

- Make athletic participation for your child and others a positive experience.

- Attempt to relieve the pressure of competition, not to increase it. A child is easily affected by outside influences.

- Be kind to your child's coach and to officials. The coach is a volunteer giving of personal time and money to provide a recreational activity for your child. The coach is providing valuable community service often without reward other than the personal satisfaction of having served the community.

- The opponents are necessary friends. Without them your child could not participate.

- Applaud good plays by your team and by members of the opposing team.

Between the exuberance of the winner and the disappointment of the loser we find a person called a referee. All of them follow the same creed to watch every move of every player and to call the game to the best of his ability.

- Do not openly question his judgment and never the honesty.

- Accept the results of fair play, integrity, and sportsmanship.

- Accept the results of each game. Encourage the child to be gracious in victory, and turn defeat to victory by working towards improvements.

Parental evaluation carries a great deal of weight with the preadolescent. The attitude shown by parents at games towards the child, the opposing team, the officials, and the coach influence the child's values and behavior in sports.

The only way to have a true friend is to be a true friend.

–Ralph Waldo Emerson

Trouble is a great sieve through which we sift our acquaintances. Those who are too big to pass through are friends.

It Is Not Easy...

To apologize,
To begin over,
To be unselfish,
To take advice,
To admit an error,
To face a sneer,
To be charitable,
To keep on trying,
To be considerate,
To avoid mistakes,
To endure success,
To profit by mistakes,
To forgive and forget,
To think and then act,
To keep out of the rut,
To make the best of little,
To subdue an unruly temper,
To shoulder a deserved blame,
To recognize the silver lining—
But it always pays, try it!

It is chance that makes siblings but hearts that make friends.

Have respect for everyone and remember everyone is different.

Horse sense is what stops a horse from betting on people.

Keep friendships in constant repair...

Our real task on Earth will be to love those we don't have to.

The only exercise some folks get is jumping to conclusions.

A closed mind is usually empty...because it won't allow anything to enter.

Hardening of the heart ages more people quickly than hardening of the arteries.

Be slow in choosing a friend, slower in changing.

Trust is the greatest gift one person can give another.

Behind an able human there are always other able humans.

One of the mysteries of life is how the boy who wasn't good enough to marry the daughter can be the father of the smartest grandchild in the world.

Mistrust the one who finds everything good, the one who finds everything evil, and still more, the one who is indifferent to everything.

Just Tell Him Now

If with pleasure you are viewing any work a man is doing,
If you like him or you love him, tell him now;
Don't withhold your approbation till the parson makes oration,
And he lies with snowy lilies o'er his brow;
For no matter how you shout it, he won't really care about it,
He won't know how many teardrops you have shed.
If you think some praise is due him,
Now's the time to slip it to him,
For he cannot read his tombstone when he's dead.

More than fame and more than money,
Is the comment, kind and sunny,
And the hearty, warm approval of a friend;
For it gives to life a savor, makes you richer, stronger braver—
Gives you heart and hope and courage to the end.
It he earns your praise, bestow it;
If you like him, let him know it;
Let the word of true encouragement be said.
Do not wait till life is over and he's underneath the clover,
For he cannot read his tombstone when he's dead.

Tact is the art of making a point without making an enemy.

I may not be easy to reach, but I may be worth it.

You'll never know how much I appreciate you, because I'll probably never tell you.

Do unto others as if others were you.

When it comes to helping others, some people stop at nothing.

Love reduces *friction* to a *fraction*.

Time wounds all heels.

A song's not a song til you sing it,
A bell's not a bell til you ring it,
Love in your heart wasn't put there to stay,
Love isn't love til you give it away.

—Oscar Hammerstein

Friendships multiply joys and divide griefs.

—H. G. Bohn

One moment of patience may ward off a great disaster; one moment of impatience may ruin a whole life.

Don't walk in front of me; I may not follow.
Don't walk behind me; I may not lead.
But walk beside me, and be my friend.

The world is as vast as the imagination. Most people choose to live in a half-vast world!

Thoughts...

Did you ever stop to think
When you're feeling kind of blue
That the one who sits beside you
May have troubles worse than you?

Just try a friendly gesture
Stick out a helping hand.
You may help to build a castle
Where before stood ebbing sand.

As you cheer your saddened neighbor
So your troubles lighter seem
You have driven out the darkness
With friendship's golden beam.

A friendly word costs nothing
Yet has power hundred fold
And worth more to be a brother
Than pocket full of gold.

Remember this when driving
With care and courtesy
Lives saved by pleasant actions
May be his or even thee.

None goes his way alone. All that we send into the lives of others comes back into our own.

—Edwin Markham

A Friend in Need

"A friend in need," my neighbor said to me, "A friend indeed is what I mean to be. In time of trouble I will come to you, and in the hour of need, you'll find me true." I thought a bit, and took him by the hand. "My friend," said I, "You do not understand the inner meaning of that simple rhyme: a friend is what the heart needs all the time."

There is no such thing as a good child. There is no such thing as a bad child. There are only healthy or unhealthy children, happy or unhappy children. Always strive to make your children healthy and happy and you won't have to worry about their behavior or their success in life. Their happy self-image will assure both.

Teachers who avoid haste and blame, teachers who come to class with a well-prepared lesson plan that moves students along easily to mastery of the subject, teachers who smile and are quick to praise, help their pupils achieve success and build a positive image of themselves as students.

Love is kind, never jealous…never haughty or selfish. If you love someone you will be loyal, no matter what the cost. You will always believe in him, always expect the best, and always stand your ground defending him.

–I Corinthians 13

All of us are born for a reason, but not all of us discover it. Success in life has nothing to do with what you gain or accomplish for yourself, it's what you do for others.

The three hardest tasks in the world are neither physical feats nor intellectual achievements. They are, instead, moral acts: to return love for hate, to include the excluded, and to say, "I was wrong."

–Sidney J. Harris

Be interested—don't try to be interesting.

Be pleasing—don't expect to be pleased.

Be lovable—don't wait to be loved.

Be helpful—don't ask to be helped.

Be entertaining—don't wait to be entertained.

People are lonely because they build walls instead of bridges.

–Joseph Newton

Happiness Is...

Happiness is an agreeable condition of the soul arising from good luck, good fortune, or joyful satisfaction. It is also a feeling arising from the consciousness of well being...or of enjoyment.

Happiness is the product of thought. It is contentment illuminated. It is expression of the soul...impression of the heart...and enlightenment of feeling. The quality of happiness is the brightness of the face. Those who are happy bring happiness into the lives of others.

The supreme happiness of life is to know that we are loved...and those who reap enjoyment of this love have comfort, prosperity, and the fulfillment of the most cherished desire—contentment.

A happy person will give his or her best at all times, in all situations. He or she will try to turn sorrow into joy. You can rely on the truly happy when in need.

Happiness is often governed by health. Ill health or a discontented state of mind are foes of happiness. In some measure everyone is seeking happiness...but too m any mistake pleasure and revelry as a means to that end. If we want happiness, we must help others. Selfish people are never really happy. Those who try to satisfy discontent or expect satisfaction when they entrust their happiness to others are often disappointed.

If we have the desire to accept it, prosperity of mind and social happiness are ours.

The world would be brighter and better if we were all happy and cheerful, not only for our own satisfaction, but for the happiness of others.

–Vivian M. Snow

Life is like an onion; you peel it off one layer at a time and, sometimes, you weep.

A HAPPY family is an early heaven.

Legacy for a Child

I would not leave you riches,
For that you can amass:
But I small point to you the beauty
In a slender blade of grass.

I would not leave you power,
For power walks alone:
But I shall teach you brotherhood
And kindness that I've known.

I would not leave you sweet content,
For I would have you climb:
So I shall lift your face to stars
Where heaven's blessings shine.

I would not leave you much of worth
According to the men on earth:
For I…with hope and faith as themes…
Endow you with my wealth of dreams.

–Merry Browne

True happiness is found in making others happy.

Find out where you can render a service, and then render it. The rest is up to the Lord.
–S. S. Kresge

No one cares how much you know, until they know how much you care.
–Don Swartz

What we have done for ourselves alone dies with us. What we have done for others remains and is immortal.

–Albert Pike

A Story about a Fig Tree

A nobleman was riding along a road and saw an old man digging in his garden. Beside the man lay a sapling ready to be planted. The nobleman called out, "What kind of tree are you planting?"

"A fig tree," replied the old man.

"A fig tree! How old are you?" cried the nobleman.

"I am 90," came the answer.

"You are 90 years old and you plant a tree which will take years and years to bear fruit?"

"Tell me," said the old man, "did you eat figs when you were young?"

"Certainly, why?"

"Who do you think planted the tree from which those gifts were obtained?"

The nobleman hesitated. "I have no idea."

"You see, sir, our forefathers planted trees for us to enjoy, and I am doing the same for those who will come along after me. How else can I repay my debt to those who lived before me?"

Friendship is the feeling you possess for a particular person, unique from all other persons. It is a very beautiful and intimate relationship, which is destroyed if it is bestowed casually. To be able to say that you have a friend is to know that there is one person to whom your affairs are as important as his own, on whose aid and counsel and affection you can rely in all times of trouble and distress, to whose aid you will fly the moment you hear he needs your help. It is impossible for any man or woman to feel like that for more than a few persons.

–John Ervin

Generalizations are always wrong.

There Are Nine Requisites for Contented Living:

Health enough to make work a pleasure; *wealth* enough to support your needs; *strength* enough to battle with difficulties and overcome them; *grace* enough to confess your sins and forsake them; *patience* enough to toil until some good is accomplished; *charity* enough to see some good in your neighbors; *love* enough to move you to be useful and helpful to others; *faith* enough to make real the things of God; and *hope* enough to remove all anxious fears of the future.

The best and most beautiful things in the world cannot be seen or even touched. They must be felt with the heart.

–Helen Keller

I'm convinced that every boy, in his heart, would rather steal second base than an automobile.

–Thomas Clark

A New Start

I will start anew this morning with a higher, fairer creed.
I will cease to stand complaining of my ruthless neighbor's greed;
I will cease to sit pining while my duty's call is clear;
I will waste no moment whining, and my heart shall know no fear.
I will look sometimes about me for the things that merit praise;
I will search for hidden beauties that elude the grumbler's gaze.
I will try to find contentment in the paths that I must tread;
I will cease to have resentment when another moves ahead.
I will not be swayed by envy when my rival's strength is shown;
I will not deny his or her merit, but I'll strive to prove my own.
I will try to see the beauty spread before me, rain or shine;
I will cease to preach your duty, and be more concerned with mine.

People Liked Him

People liked him, not because
He was rich or known to fame;
He had never won applause
As a star in any game.
He had not a brilliant style,
He had not a forceful way,
But he had a gentle smile
And a kindly word to say.

Never arrogant or proud,
On he went with manner mild;
Never quarrelsome or loud,
Just as simple as a child;
Honest, patient, brave and true;
Thus he lived from day to day,
Doing what he found to do
In a cheerful sort of way.

Wasn't one to boast of gold
Or belittle it with sneers,
Didn't change from hot to cold,
Kept his friends throughout the years,
Sort of man you like to meet
Any time or any place.
There was always something sweet
And refreshing in his face.

Sort of man you'd like to be;
Balanced well and truly square;
Patient in adversity,
Generous when his skies were fair.
Never lied to friend or foe,
Never rash in word or deed,
Quick to come and slow to go
In a neighbor's time of need.

Never rose to wealth or fame,
Simply lived, and simply died,
But the passing of his name
Left a sorrow, far and wide.

So long as we love, we serve. So long as we are loved by others I would almost say we are indispensable; and no one is useless while he or she has a friend.

On this day...mend a quarrel. Search out a forgotten friend. Dismiss suspicion and replace it with trust. Write a letter to a distant friend. Share some treasure. Give a soft answer. Encourage youth. Manifest your loyalty in a word or deed.

Keep a promise. Find the time. Forego a grudge. Forgive an enemy. Listen. Apologize if you were wrong. Try to understand. Flout envy. Examine your demands on others. Think first of someone else. Appreciate, be kind, be gentle. Laugh a little more.

Deserve confidence. Take up arms against malice. Decry complacency. Express your gratitude. Gladden the heart of a child. Take pleasure in the beauty and wonder of the earth.

Influence

Our lives will touch so many lives
Before the day is done,
Leave many marks for right or wrong
By the things that we have done.

Each new day we should make with this
And then in earnest pray,
"Lord, let my life help other lives
That shall be met today."

Everything comes if one will only wait. I have brought myself by long meditation to the conviction that a human being with a settled purpose must accomplish it, and that nothing can resist a will that will stake even existence for its fulfillment.

You must like people for what they are, not because they are the sort of people you like.

Favor

A favor is that kindly deed,
Beyond a friendly smile,
That comforts someone else on earth,
And makes this life worthwhile.
It may involve a fortune,
Or the fraction of a cent,
Or just some little effort that
Is generously spent.
We may be asked to do it or
The thought may be our own,
In any case, it is the way
Our charity is shown.
It is a little sacrifice
That we are glad to make
To brighten up the sky a bit
For someone else's sake.
And often we consider it
A privilege to extend,
Because there is no greater deed
Than helping out a friend.

—James J. Metcalf

Time isn't holding us, time isn't after us. Same as it ever was.

—D. Byrne

When we are confused by the world we can gain a renewed sense of security from seeing the light in the eyes of a happy, trusting child.

Last night our high-school band played Beethoven. Beethoven lost.

Young Peoples' Bill of Responsibilities

To my country, my parents, and myself—That I may:

Honor my parents, my elders and my teachers.

Take care of my body, mind and spirit.

Improve myself through education, in preparation for the future.

Perform my work to the best of my ability.

Develop high moral principles and the courage to live by them.

Grow in character and ability as I grow in size.

Respect the rights and feelings of others.

Be honest with myself and others in everything I say and do.

Set a good example so others may enjoy and profit from my company.

Obey the laws of society and live in harmony with others.

Preserve and support our American way of life and the government of our people.

Keep in mind that I was not put on this earth to amuse myself or simply enjoy the fruits of the labors of others. I shall endeavor to be of service to my fellow man and leave the world a better place than I found it.

If you have a goal in life that requires a lot of energy, that incurs a great deal of interest and that is a challenge to you, you will always look forward to waking up to see what the new day brings.

If you find a person in your life that understands you completely, that shares your ideas and that believes in everything you do, you will always look forward to the night because you will never be lonely.

—Susan Polis Schutz

We all need to surround ourselves with friends and family, but in the final analysis we are totally dependent on our own inner resources. We are the one person we can count on to be with us for the entire journey. The more we like that person, the happier we will be during the times we are alone.

Four Characteristics Usually Found in Those Who Impact Our Lives

Consistency. These folk are not restless flashes in the pan, here today, gone tomorrow. Neither are they given to fads and gimmicks. Those who impact lives stay at the task with reliable regularity. They seem unaffected by the fickle winds of change. They're consistent.

Authenticity. Probe all you wish, try all you like to find hypocrisy, and you search in vain. People who impact others are real to the core—no alloy covered over with a brittle layer of chrome—but solid, genuine stuff right down to the nubbies. They're authentic.

Unselfishness. Mustn't forget this one! Hands down it's there every time. Those who impact us the most watch out for themselves the least. They notice our needs and reach out to help, honestly concerned about our welfare. Their least-used words are "I," "me," "my," and "mine." They're unselfish.

Tirelessness. With relentless determination they spend themselves. They refuse to quit. Possessing an enormous amount of enthusiasm for their labor, they press on regardless of the odds…virtually unconcerned with the obstacles. Actually, they are like pioneers—resilient and rugged. They're tireless.

You have no enemies, you say?
Alas, my friend, the boast is poor;
He who has mingled in the fray
Of duty, that the brave endure,
Must have made foes! If you have none,
Small is the work that you have done.
You've hit no traitor on the hip,
You've dashed no cup from perjured lip,
You've never turned the wrong to right,
You've been a coward in the fight.

–Charles MacKay

It doesn't matter who my father was; it matters who I remember he was.

The Best Memory System

Forget each kindness that you do
As soon as you have done it.
Forget the praise that falls on you
The moment you have won it.
Forget the slander that you hear
Before you can repeat it.

Forget each slight, each spite,
Each sneer, wherever you may meet it.
Remember every kindness done
To you, whatever its measure.
Remember praise by others won
And pass it on with pleasure.

Remember every promise made
And keep it to the letter.
Remember those who lend you aid
And be a grateful debtor.
Remember all the happiness
That comes your way in living.

Forget each worry and distress,
Be hopeful and forgiving.
Remember good, remember truth,
Remember heaven is above you.
And you will find, through age and youth,
That many hearts will love you.

Who touches a Boy, by the Master's plan Is shaping the course of the future man. Father or mother or teacher or priest, Friend or stranger or saint or beast, Is dealing with one who is living seed, And may be a man whom the world shall need.

In order to have an enemy one must be somebody.

—Swetchine

Deciding Right From Wrong

Does the course of action you plan to follow seem logical and reasonable? Never mind what anyone else has to say, does it make sense to you? If it does, it is probably right.

Does it pass the test of sportsmanship? In other words, if everyone followed this same course of action would the results be beneficial for all?

Where will your plan of action lead? How will it affect others? What will it do to you?

Will you think well of yourself when you look back at what you have done?

Try to separate yourself from the problem. Pretend, for one moment, it is the problem of the person you most admire. Ask yourself how that person would handle it.

Hold up the final decision to the flaring light of publicity. Would you want your family and friends to know what you have done? The decisions we make in the hope that no one will find out are usually wrong.

–Dr. Harry E. Fosdick

Dad's 91st Birthday Was Sad

Yesterday was an old man's birthday. He was 91. He awakened earlier than usual, bathed, shaved, and put on his best clothes. Surely they would come today, he thought. He didn't take his daily walk to the gas station to visit the old timers of the community, because he wanted to be right there when they came.

He sat on the front porch with a clear view of the road so he could see them coming. Surely they would come today. He decided to skip his noon nap because he wanted to be up when they came. He has six children.

Two of his daughters and their married children live within four miles. They hadn't been to see him for such a long time, but today was his birthday. Surely they would come today.

At suppertime he refused to cut the cake and asked that the ice cream be left in the freezer. He wanted to wait and have dessert with them when they came.

About nine o'clock, he went to his room and got ready for bed. His last words before turning out the lights were, "Promise to wake me up when they come." It was his birthday and he was 91.

If I command the language ever so perfectly and speak as a pundit, and yet have not the love that grips the heart, I am nothing. If I possess decorations and diplomas and am proficient in recent methods and have not the touch of understanding love, I am nothing.

If I am able to best my opponents in arguments so as to make fools of them, and have not the wooing note, I am nothing. If I have all faith and great ideals and magnificent plans and wonderful visions, and have not the love that sweats and bleeds and weeps and prays and pleads, I am nothing.

If I surrender all prospects and, leaving home and friends and comforts, to give myself to the vain, glorious sacrifice of a missionary career, and turn sour and selfish amid the daily annoyances and personal slights of a missionary life, and though I give my body to be consumed in the heat and sweat and mildew of India, and have not the love that yields its rights, its coveted leisure, its pet plans, I am nothing. *Nothing.* Virtue has ceased to emanate from me.

If I can heal all manner of sickness and disease, but wound hearts and hurt feelings for want of love that is kind, I am nothing. If I write books and publish articles that set the world agape and fail to transcribe the word of the cross in the language of love, I am nothing. Worse, I may be competent, busy, fussy, punctilious, and well-equipped, but like the church at Laodicea—nauseating to Christ.

Kind hearts are the gardens,

Kind thoughts are the roots,

Kind words are the flowers

Kind deeds are the fruits.

Champions are mythical. The real champions are those who live through what they are taught in their homes and their churches. The attitude that 'we've got to win' in sports must be changed. Teach your youngsters, who are the future hope of America, the importance of love, respect, dedication, determination, self-sacrifice, self-discipline and good attitude. That's the road up the ladder to championships.

—Jesse Owens

Dear Son,

I suppose a boy your age often wonders how he stacks up in the eyes of his dad. If my eyes have not already told you, son, perhaps, risking sentimentalism, I can express my feelings in this letter.

How can I adequately express the feeling of pride I have for you not only as an athlete in uniform but as an individual out of it? The pride that has built up over a period of years in your dedication to athletics.

You've outgrown me by a couple of inches now, but it seems like yesterday that you sat on my lap watching the games on TV. I explained the games to you then, now you explain them to me.

Through the years I've kept my eye on you. I've watched you develop, grow and participate, and I've noticed many things.

I watched you devote your life to rigid training and clean living. I have seen you develop into a boy with spirit, confidence, and with a will to win. Yet, along with this grew modesty, humility, and respect for the other guy along with a compassion for fellow players.

I've seen you cry and suffer silently in defeat and exalt in victory. There was no need to look at me in embarrassment, son, when you thought you did not perform well, because I knew you were doing the best you could. You always did the best you could.

And yet, there were the many times your play was outstanding—the homerun to win the ballgame, the winning bucket, the second effort for a touchdown, and the final spurt to win the race. At times I cried too—but with tears of pride.

Of all life has to offer, of all that's great and true, that which means the most to me is being friends with you.

We all find time to do what we really want to do.

—William Feather

If you're looking for love, bring a little bit with you.

I've seen you get a few knocks—at times helped off the field. And I've seen signs of pain on your face. I felt that pain too, son. We used a lot of liniment nursing you through your aches and pains.

I've swelled with pride when the crowd gave you a standing ovation in appreciation of your efforts and performance. And how proud I was to be your father after a coach's comment, "He's the kind of son I would like to have!"

Then the compliments from different walks of life—the dentist with questions about next week's game and the grocer inquiring about your health. I've seen your mother's looks of pride and I've heard your brothers and sisters boast about you. You've earned these compliments, son, not only with your fine efforts, but with your sportsmanship. I've seen you place yourself in the doorway of the opposing players' locker room to shake their hands, in victory or defeat, and I've heard you pass a few kind words to your opponent's coach.

Never once have I seen you deliberately try to hurt an opponent nor take advantage of an unfair situation. With all of this, you have earned the respect of coaches, officials, and opposing players.

It isn't that important whether you make All-Conference or Most Valuable. The point is that up to now you've played well and lived well—a step toward desirable and successful adulthood. To say I'm proud of you, son, is putting it mildly!

Love,

Your Dad

A father who makes his children think he is smarter or stronger than he really is may command their respect for a few years, but honesty and humility are the only qualities that gain enduring love.

When I give, I give myself.

—Walt Whitman

Parents Can Give Positive Self-Image

By Dr. David Goodman

Are you happy because you are successful or are you successful because you are happy?

This is no mere play on words. The answer has great psychological significance, especially for child training, whether at home or in school.

The answer is that you are successful because you are happy. Your brain and nervous system are a serving mechanism. They promote whatever idea of yourself you entertain in your mind. If you have a happy, self-confident image of yourself, that's what they will work to promote. If you have a fearful image of yourself, that will be what they will promote.

Imagination is all. Your imagination makes your fate, and the fate of your children. You can give your children a happy, self-confident image of themselves by affording them love with liberty. Loved children feel secure, at ease in the universe. They also feel that they are important enough to merit their parents' affection and praise. If their parents encourage their self-reliance by avoiding the egotistical urge to do for them what they can do for themselves, they will grow up strong, competent, happy adults.

All this is easy, especially if you have a good image of yourself as a parent, but remember always: patronizing isn't love.

(The Canadian Mental Health Association contributed this wonderfully wise summary of child training.)

7

Losing

❖

Quitting

Wealth lost, little lost;
Honor lost, much lost;
Courage lost, all lost.

O Lord, help my words to be gracious and tender
today, for tomorrow I may have to eat them.

Photo: Holly Stein/Getty Images

Too many folks think they can push themselves forward by patting themselves on the back.

Don't Quit

When things go wrong, as they sometimes will, when the road you're trudging seems all uphill, when the funds are low and the debts are high, and you want to smile but you have to sigh, when care is pressing you down a bit—rest if you must, but don't you quit.

Life is queer with its twists and turns. As every one of us sometimes learns. And many a fellow turns about when he might have won had it stuck it out. Don't give up though the pace seems slow—you may succeed with another blow.

Often the goal is nearer than it seems to a faint and faltering man; often the struggler has given up when he might have captured the victor's cup; and he learned too late when the night came down, how close he was to the golden crown.

Success is failure turned inside out—the silver tint of the clouds of doubt, and when you never can tell how close you are, it may be near when it seems afar; so stick to the fight when you're hardest hit—it's when things seem worst, you mustn't quit.

Any time the going seems easier, you had better check to see that you're not going downhill.

Studying history will not only teach you how others succeeded but also why they failed.

Too many of us conduct our lives on the cafeteria plan—SELF-SERVICE ONLY.

Keep A Goin'...

You play another team today, Keep a goin'.

You've been playing pretty well,
Now don't take a breathing spell,
Give the stands a chance to yell, Keep a goin'.

If you strike a tougher bunch, Keep a goin'.

You only need a harder punch, Keep a goin'.

Taint no use to stand and whine
When they're coming through the line,
Hitch up your trousers and climb. Keep a goin'.

If the other team's on top, Keep a goin'.

That's just the time you must not stop, Keep a goin'.

S'pose they stop most every play,
One good long run may win the day,
You might grab a pass and get away, Keep a goin'.

When it seems the game is lost, Keep a goin'.
Do not quit at any cost, Keep a goin'.

Don't ever think that you can't win it,
A fighting team is always in it,
So don't let up a single minute. Keep a goin'.

Prolonged idleness paralyzes initiative.

There is no mistake so great as the mistake of not going on...

Play The Game

Quit your crabbing, quit your gabbing, just get in and play the game.
Quit your fussing, quit your cussing, do honor to your name.
It's no use to be dejected, just get in and be respected,
And do more than is expected, play the game.

Quit your growling, quit your howling, make a victory gleam.
Win the game, be winners all. Do your best at every call.
Be a fighter 'till you fall—play the game.

Quit your dragging, quit your nagging. Help your men along.
Do some coaxing, do some hoaxing, show them you are strong.
Slap your teammate on the back, make him feel it—make it smack,
Let him know your pop's not slack, play the game.

Quit your slugging, start to lugging, work hard on court or field.
You're a licker, you're a sticker, never known to yield.
Don't you for a moment loiter, you're a winner, an exploiter,
Show them how to reconnoiter—play the game.

I'd rather see a lesson than to hear one any day,

I'd rather you'd walk with me than to merely show the way.

The eye's a better teacher and more willing than the ear, and counsel is confusing but examples always clear.

The best of all the teachers are the ones who live the deeds, to see the good in action is what everybody needs.

I soon can learn to do it if you let me see it done, I can see your hand in action but your tongue too fast may run.

And the counsel you are giving may be very fine and true, but I'd rather get my lesson by observing what you do!

The Coach

A coach there was and he made his prayer
(Even as you and I)
To a bat and a ball and years of strife
Only to feel the Critics' knife
But the fool called it his way of life.
(Even as you and I)

Oh the years we waste and the tears we waste
And the work of head and hand
Belong to the poor coach who did not know
(And now he knows he will never know)
And cannot understand

A coach there was and the time he spent
(Even as you and I)
To teach a quarterback with good intent
But the boy called a play that was not meant
(Even as you and I)

Oh the play we lost and the game we lost
Though excellent things were planned
Belongs to the Coach who didn't know why
And now we know he will never know why
And cannot understand

The Coach was stripped of all his pride
(Even as you and I)
When the fans of the team threw him aside
Though some of him lived, most of him died
(Even as you and I)

Oh, why can't the game ever be won
With a last minute hit or goal
And isn't the blame and isn't the shame
That strings the Coach like a red-hot coal
It's coming to know he will never know
And will never understand…

If you are made of the right stuff, a hard fall results in a high bounce.

The minute you get the idea you're indispensable, you aren't.

It is defeat that turns bone to flint, it is defeat that turns muscle to gristle, it is defeat that makes us invincible.

From the Camp of the Beaten

I have learned something well worthwhile
That victory could not bring—
To wipe the blood from my mouth and smile
Where none can see the sting.
I can walk, head up, while my heart is down
From the beating that brought its good,
And that means more than the champion's crown
Who is taking the easier road.
I have learned something worth far more
Than victory brings to men;
Battered and beaten, bruised and sore,
I can still come back again;
Crowded back in the hard, tough race,
I've found that I have the heart
To look raw failure in the face
And train for another start.
Winners who wear the victor's wreath,
Looking for softer ways,
Watch for my blade as it leaves the sheath,
Sharpened on rougher days.
Trained upon pain and punishment,
I've groped my way through the night,
But the flag still flies from my battle tent
And I've only begun to fight…

Experience is a wonderful thing. It enables you to recognize a mistake when you make it again.

A parrot talks much but flies little.

When Things Go Wrong

I count it best, when things go wrong, to hum a tune and sing a song; a heavy heart means sure defeat, but joy is victory replete.

If skies are cloudy, count the gain, new life depends upon the rain; the cuckoo carols loud and long when clouds hang low and things go wrong.

When things go wrong, remember then the happy heart has strength of ten; forget the sorrow, sing a song—it makes all right when things go wrong.

–Charles Henry Chelsey

Some people are built upside down—their feet smell and their nose runs.

If you think you're confused, consider poor Columbus. He didn't know where he was going. When he got there, he didn't know where he was. And when he got back he didn't know where he had been.

The reason some people do not succeed is because their wishbone is where their *backbone* ought to be.

Stick It Out

When your world's about to fall,
And your back's against the wall,
When you're facing wild retreat and utter rout;
When it seems that naught can stop it,
All your pleas and plans can't prop it
Get a grip upon yourself and—stick it out!
Any craven fool can quit,
But the ones with pluck and grit,
Will hold until the very final shout;
In the snarling teeth of sorrow
They will laugh and say "Tomorrow
The luck will change—I guess I'll stick it out."
The luck does change; you know it;
All the records prove and show it,
And the ones who win are ones who strangle doubt,
Who hesitate nor swerve,
Who have grit and guts and nerve,
And whose motto is: Play hard, and stick it out.
And you think you can't last long,
So you, when things go wrong,
That you've got to quit nor wait for the final bout;
Smile, smile at your beholders,
Clench your teeth and square your shoulders
And you'll win if you but stick it out!
❖

The stands are for spectators, not the playing field.

—Frank Broyles

When you think you're at the end of your rope—tie a knot in it and hang on.

You can't keep trouble from coming, but you needn't give it a chair to sit on.

If you indulge in self-pity, the only sympathy you can expect is from the same source.

Life is not easy for any of us, but it is a continued challenge, and it is up to us to be cheerful and to be strong, so that those who depend on us may draw strength from our example.

The Indispensable Man

Sometime when you're feeling important, sometime when your ego's in bloom, sometime when you take it for granted you're the best qualified in the room. Sometime when you feel your going would leave an unfillable hole, just follow this simple instruction and see how it humbles your soul.

Take a bucket and fill it with water, put your hand in up to your wrist, take it out—and the hole that's remaining is a measure of how you'll be missed. You can splash all you please as you enter, you can stir up the water galore, but stop, and you'll see in a minute that it looks quite the same as before.

There's a moral in this quaint expression, just do the best that you can, be proud of yourself, but remember there is no indispensable man.

A person is about as big as the things that make him or her angry.

Following the path of least resistance is what makes people and rivers crooked.

Don't leave any regrets on the field.

If lessons are learned in defeat as they say, our team is really getting a great education.
—Murray Warmath

He failed in business in '32.

He ran as a state legislator and lost in '32.

He tried business again and failed in '33.

His sweetheart died in '35.

He had a nervous breakdown in '36.

He ran for state elector in '40 after he regained his health.

He was defeated for congress in '43, defeated again for congress in '48, defeated when he ran for senate in '55 and defeated for vice president of the United States in '56.

He ran for the senate again in '58 and lost.

This man never quit.

He kept trying til the last.

In 1860, this man, Abraham Lincoln, was elected President of the United States of America.

Crying over spilt milk does nothing but make a bigger mess to clean up.

The best eraser in the world is a good night's sleep.

We all make mistakes—especially those who do things.

People do not fail, they just give up easily.

Four things never come back—the spoken word, the sped arrow, the past life, and the neglected opportunity.

It's a lot tougher to be a football coach than a president. You've got four years as a president, and they guard you. A coach doesn't have anyone to protect him when things go wrong.

–Harry Truman

Quitting is easy, fighting is hard
Quitting is losing, fighting is winning.

–Buck Nystrom

Conceit is a queer disease. It makes everyone sick except the one who has it.

When looking back, usually I'm more sorry for the things I didn't do than for the things I shouldn't have done.

Why Worry?

There are only two things to worry about; either you are well or you are sick. If you are well, then there is nothing to worry about. But if you are sick, there are two things to worry about: either you will get well, or you will die. If you get well, there is nothing to worry about. If you die, there are only two things to worry about: either you will go to Heaven or Hell. If you go to Heaven, there is nothing to worry about. But if you go to Hell, you'll be so busy shaking hands with friends you won't have time to worry.

There's no thrill in easy sailing, when the skies are clear and blue. There's no joy in merely doing things, which anyone can do. But there is some satisfaction that is mighty sweet to take, when you reach a destination that you thought you couldn't make!

All for the Best

Sometimes the sky is overcast…And I am feeling blue…And as the hours wander by…I know not what to do…And sometimes there is tragedy…To meet me at the door…And I must wonder whether life…Is worth my fighting for…But always there is some way out…And I have come to know…That brighter things will comfort me…In just a day or so…And I have learned that what is past…Was purposeful and good…But in my bed of bitterness…It was misunderstood…There is a certain destiny…In every human quest…Because when anything goes wrong…It happens for the best.

What Are You Doing Now?

It matters not if you lost the fight and were badly beaten too.
It matters not if you failed outright in the things you tried to do.
It matters not if you toppled down from the azure heights of blue,
But what are you doing now?

It matters not if your plans were foiled and your hopes have fallen through.
It matters not if your chance was spoiled for the gain almost in view.
It matters not if you missed the goal though you struggled brave and true…
But what are you doing now?

It matters not if your fortune's gone and your fame has vanished too.
It matters not if a cruel world's score be directed straight at you.
It matters not if the worst has come and your dreams have not come true…
But what are you doing now?

–R. Rhodes Stabley

When success turns a person's head, he's facing failure.

Unless you try to do something beyond what you have already done and mastered, you will never grow...

A job done poorly stands as a witness against the one who did it.

Success is never permanent. And fortunately, neither is failure...

We are all manufacturers. Some make good, others make trouble, and still others make excuses.

Setbacks never whip a fighter.

Any fool can criticize, condemn, and complain—and most fools do!
—Dale Carnegie

Nothing is opened by mistake as often as one's mouth.

It is not because things are difficult that we do not dare; it is because we do not dare that they are difficult.
—Seneca

Macho does not prove mucho.

Peace comes not from the absence of conflict in life but from the ability to cope with it.

If everything is going your way, you are probably heading in the wrong direction.

I cannot give you a formula for success, but I can give you the formula for failure, which is: *Try to please everybody.*

–Herbert Bayard Swope

Some people who slap you on the back are trying to help you swallow what they just told you.

Failure is something you know in your heart. Success is something that lies in the eye of the beholder.

Excuses are like belly buttons: everybody has one.

Every great improvement has come after related failures. Virtually nothing comes out right the first time. Failures, repeated failures, are fingerposts on the road to achievement.

–Charles F. Kettering

The trouble with this world is that too many people try to go through life with a catcher's mitt on both hands.

Defeat must be *faced*, but it need not be *final*.

There is no sadder sight than a young pessimist.

–Mark Twain

To him who tries and fails and quits—

I am the foul blow.

But, to him who in defeat, the lessons of life would learn—

I lead through darkness and disaster

To where the scarlet lights of triumph burn.

After all is said and done, there's a lot more said than done.

If things are not going well with you, begin correcting the situation by carefully examining the service you are rendering, and especially the spirit in which you are rendering it.

–Roger Babson

Giving up is the ultimate tragedy.

–Robert J. Donovan

Don't waste time in doubts and fears; spend yourself in the work before you, well assured that the right performance of this hour's duties will be the best preparation for the hours or ages that follow it.

–Ralph Waldo Emerson

The only things that evolve by themselves in an organization are disorder, friction, and malperformance.

Most anything in life is easier to get into than out of.

People begin cutting their wisdom teeth the first time they bite off more than they can chew.

If you never take a chance, you will never be defeated. But you will never accomplish anything either.

Press On

Nothing in the world can take the place of persistence.
Talent will not; nothing is more common than unsuccessful individuals with talent.
Genius will not; unrewarded genius is almost a proverb.
Education will not; the world is full of educated derelicts.
Persistence and determination alone are omnipotent.

Everyone will get beat sometime physically but a champion seldom gets beat mentally.

–Chuck Knoll

When you imagine that you have attained perfection your decline begins.

When the Pressure's On

How do you act when the pressure's on,
When the chance for victory's almost gone,
When Fortune's star has refused to shine,
When the ball is on your five-yard line?

How do you act when the going's rough,
Does your spirit lag when breaks are tough?
Or, is there in you a flame that glows
Brighter as fiercer the battle grows?

How hard, how long will you fight the foe?
That's what the world would like to know!
Cowards can fight when they're out ahead!
The uphill grind shows a thoroughbred!

You wish for success? Then tell me, son,
How do you act when the pressure's on?

A diamond cannot be polished without friction, nor a person perfected without trials.

When the outlook is bad, try the uplook.

There is so much that is bad in the best of us, and so much that is good in the worst of us, that it doesn't behoove any of us, to talk about the rest of us.

If you never have failed, it's an even guess you never have won a high success.

Are you part of the *problem* or part of the *solution*?

The load of tomorrow, added to that of yesterday, carried today, makes the strongest falter.

—Sir William Osler

Luck is always against the one who depends on it.

Failure is the line of least persistence.

Some people are so busy learning the tricks of the trade that they never learn the trade.

With the application of our abilities as one team, we can make our own "breaks." We can create the "luck" that can be so elusive. Four key aspects of teamwork do the job:

Loyalty

Unselfishness

Cooperation

Kindness

It Might Have Been Worse

Sometimes I pause and sadly think
Of the things that might have been,
Of the golden chances I let slip by,
And which never returned again.

Think of the joys that might have been mine:
The prizes I almost won,
The goals I missed by a mere hair's breadth
And the things I might have done.

It fills me with gloom when I ponder thus,
Till I look on the other side,
How I might have been completely engulfed
By misfortune's surging tide.

The unknown dangers lurking about—
Which I passed safely through
The evils and sorrows that I've been spared
Pass plainly now in review.

So when I am downcast and feeling sad,
I repeat over and over again,
Things are far from being as bad
As they easily might have been.

—G. T. Russell

Life is a mixture of sunshine and rain,
Teardrops and laughter, pleasure and pain.
We can't have all bright days but it's certainly true
There was never a cloud that the sun didn't shine through!

Lack of something to feel important about is almost the greatest tragedy one can have.

The Laggard's Excuse

They worked by day
And toiled by night,
They gave up play
And some delight.

Dry books they'd read
New things to learn
And forged ahead,
Success to earn.

They plodded on
With faith and pluck,
And when they won
People called it luck.

Those who make the worst of their time are the first to complain of its shortness.

You may make mistakes, but you are not a failure until you start blaming someone else.

In the Prison Chronicle, noted Russian author and Christian, Alexander Solzhenitsyn, says this about adversity:

"Don't be afraid of misfortune and do not yearn after happiness. It is, after all, all the same. The bitter doesn't last forever, and the sweet never fills the cup to overflowing. It is enough if you don't freeze in the cold and if hunger and thirst don't claw at your sides.

"If your back isn't broken, if your feet can walk, if both arms work, if both eyes can see, and if both ears can hear, then whom should you envy? And why? Our envy of others devours us most of all. Rub your eyes and purify your heart and prize above all else in the world those you love and those you wish well…"

There is a good deal of wasted talent in the world, and some of the waste comes from sheer ignorance. People simply do not know how to apply their energies.

–Gilbert Highet

The average human has 66 pounds of muscle and about 3 pounds of brains—which explains a lot of things.

A doctor's mistake is buried.

A lawyer's mistake is imprisoned.

An accountant's mistake is jailed.

A dentist's mistake is pulled.

A pharmacist's mistake is dead.

A plumber's mistake is stopped.

An electrician's mistake is shocking.

A teacher's mistake is failed.

A printer's mistake is redone.

And yours?

"People are not finished when they are defeated," he told me. "They are finished when they quit. My philosophy is that no matter how many times you are knocked down you get off that floor, even if you are bloody, battered, and beaten, and just keep slugging—providing you have something to live for.

"If you have something you believe is worth fighting for, the greatest test is not when you are standing, but when you are down on that floor. You've got to get up and start banging again. When I study men and women leaders in history, those I admire the most are those who have gone through adversity and come back. You've got to learn to survive a defeat. That's when you develop character."

The opponent who is ungracious in defeat is merely weak and small, but the one who is ungracious in victory has a fatally flawed character.

–Sidney J. Harris

I've learned that the person who says that they will meet you half way is usually a poor judge of distance.

–Roger L. Grover

I don't like to lose; I never have. I never will. The thought is repugnant to me, because defeat means only one thing: failure to meet your objective. The trouble in America today, in business, in government, and in organizations is that too many people are afraid of the active life, competition, and hard work. The result is that, in some circles, people have come to sneer at success if it means training, sacrifice, and hard work.

It's Easy to Quit...

Anyone can say, "The hill is too high" or "It's too far away."
Anyone can say, "I'm too tired to keep on," and stop halfway there. Don't be that one.

> Whenever life gives you a task to do,
> Don't stop in the middle
> See the thing through.
>
> It's easy to quit
> Any fool can explain
> To himself and his friends
> When the struggle was vain.
>
> It doesn't take brains
> When you start cutting loose
> From a difficult task
> To think up an excuse.

No trial would trouble you if you knew God's purpose in sending it.

Penalties for Wasting Time Cited

To get promoted you don't have to be best, you need only be the least worst of all known candidates at the time.

The true test of the professional is not what she knows how to do, but how she behaves when she does not know what to do.

The difference between education and experience is that education is what you get from reading the fine print, whereas experience is what you get from not reading it.

We will not learn how to create a more perfect world until we know how to live more perfectly in this imperfect world.

Those Who Fail

All honor to them who shall win the prize
The world has cried for a thousand years
But to them who try and who fail and die
I give great honor and glory and tears.

O great is the hero who wins a name
But greater many and many a time
Some pale-faced human who dies in shame
And lets God finish the thought sublime.

O great is the one with a sword undrawn
And good is the one who refrains from wine
But the one who fails and yet fights on
Lo, that one is the twin of mine.

No Scar?

Hast thou no scar?
No hidden scar on foot, or side, or hand?
I hear thee sung as mighty in the land,
I hear them paid thy bright ascendant star
Hast thou no scar?

Hast thou no wound?
Yet I was wounded by the archers, spent,
Leaned Me against a tree to die; and rent
By ravening beast that compassed Me, I swooned:
Hast thou no wound?

No wound, no scar?
Yet, as the Master shall the servant be,
And, pierced are the feet that follow Me.
But thine are whole; can one have followed far
Who has no wound and no scar?

There are Basically Four Kinds of People

First, there are the cop-outs. These people set no goals and make no decision.

Second, there are the hold-outs. They have a beautiful dream, but they're afraid to respond to its challenge because they aren't sure they can make it. These people have lost all childlike faith.

Third, there are the drop-outs. They start to make their dream come true. They know their role. They set their goals, but when the going gets tough, they quit. They don't pay the toll.

Finally, there are the all-outs. They are the people who know their role. They want and need and are going to be stars: star students, star parents, star waitresses, star coaches, star teachers. They want to shine out as an inspiration to others. They set their goals. They ask, "How can I live the one life I have and make it something beautiful for God?" Their goals are God-inspired, a team effort. The all-outs never quit. Even when the toll gets heavy, they're dedicated. They're committed.

–Robert H. Schuller

The prime difference between "sympathy" and "pity" is that we can feel the first for someone who has tried and failed, but the second only for someone who has failed to try.

A team can lose. Any team can lose, but in a sense, a very real sense, a coach never loses: The job of a coach is over and finished once the starting whistle blows. He or she knows whether he or she has won or lost before play starts.

A coach has two tasks. The minor one is to teach skills: To teach a youth how to run faster, hit harder, block better, kick farther, and jump higher.

The second task—the major task—is to make adults out of children. It's to teach an attitude of mind. It's to implant character and not simply to impart skills.

It's to teach children to play fair. It's to teach them to be humble in victory and proud in defeat. This goes without saying; but, more important, it's to teach them to live up to their potential no matter what that potential is.

It's to teach them to do their best and never be satisfied with what they are, but to strive to be as good as they can.

For a coach, the final score doesn't read so many points for my team, so many for theirs. Instead it reads: So many adults out of so many children—and this is the score in which he or she finds real joy when the last game is over.

The trouble with most people is that they think with their hopes or fears or wishes rather than with their minds.

–Walter Duranty

Anger is only one letter short of danger.

The Fear of Failure

The following are some notes from an address given to the mid-winter graduating Class of 1974 from the University of Maryland by the president of Johns Hopkins University.

I would like to talk to you for a few minutes about a subject you surely did not expect: failure. It may seem odd at this time of success and congratulations, but in my view, now is in fact the right moment.

Americans do not understand, nor do they live well, with failure. Yet it is an inevitable part of the human condition; no one can win them all. We have made a national fetish of success and victory—I think to a dangerous degree.

I believe in achievement, but I believe the crucial factor is the effort rather than the result. Who can do more than one's best? Who can ask more than to give the most one has? A successful person is one who is productive to the peak of his capacity and who is comfortable with his or her own self.

This sounds so simple, but it is not commonly accepted. Success is equated with wealth, power, prestige, and notoriety. These are dubious assets—some crave and possess them, but find no happiness or fulfillment in this application. Clearly they are not equally available to all. But a successful life is possible for each of us. My argument is that, as a people, we try to shut out the realities of failure and of death (the ultimate failure), and that this is unhealthy. Each of us will die and each of us will fail at things. Can't we admit that and live with it?

To Any Athlete

Why is it each is the last to find
That his legs are gone, that his eyes are bad,
That the quicker reflexes have left his mind,
That he hasn't the stuff that he one day had,
That lost youth mocks, and he doesn't see
The ghost of the fellow that used to be?

Caught by a stride, which they used to beat
Nailed by a punch that they used to block
Trailing the flurry of flying feet,
But dreaming still of the peaks that mock
Each is the last to learn from fate
That his story is finished and out of date.

The message of organized Christianity has been that death is a natural climax of life, not a hateful event. Failure is no disgrace. He who never failed can never have tried very hard, and how do we know our limits without failure?

I object to the notion that winning is everything. Victory may be sweet, but it is a fleeting moment. Certainly that you have done your best is durable and is the basis for self-respect, which is the ultimate in human satisfaction. Few people learn from success, but there is often much to learn from failure. Yet no one can learn from failure without admitting it first.

I believe in competition and I like to win, but I deny that the only thing that matters is winning, or that winning can be the goal of a successful life. Winning and losing are inseparable, and it is the effort involved that means much more than either.

Let me play the role assigned to me by urging the following:

- Strive for the self-respect that comes from giving your best to whatever you do, and measure success by the degree to which you are at peace with yourself.

- Accept failure as natural and unavoidable and do not allow the best that is in you to be stunted by fear of failure.

- Admit your failures easily, not only because it is neurotic to deny them, but because to fail the first time may be the best way to learn how to master the problem.

To each of you I wish a successful life of self-respect based on your best efforts.

You are a poor specimen if you can't stand the pressure of adversity.

Life is mostly froth and bubble
Two things stand as stone:
Kindness in another's trouble
Courage in your own.

Cowards can fight when they're out ahead, but the uphill grind shows the thoroughbred.

Tomorrow's Fame in Today's Lost Game

The score has gone against you
And everything looks blue;
You bow your head in bitterness
And vow your playings through;
The team that won the trophy,
You've defeated once before
But the breaks were all against you;
It's left you sick and sore.
You're tired and discouraged,
You'd like to shift the blame
To coach, umpire, or teammate
You'd like to curse the game;
But a rhyme fits through your mem'ry
To lighten the gloom you carry,
"Tomorrow's fame in today's lost game;
Defeat is just temporary."

—H. Victory

I'm not afraid of losing. I just don't want to be there when it happens.

—Duffy Daugherty

There is a time to take counsel of your fears, and there is a time to never listen to any fear.

—Gen. George S. Patton

8

Teamwork

❖

Unity

No team can ever be whipped if they hang tough together and refuse to be beaten.

Photo: David Rogers/Getty Images

No team has a corner on hard work, desire and enthusiasm.

–Duffy Daugherty

I carry a link in my pocket
A simple reminder to me
Of the fact that I am a team member
No matter where I may be.

This little link is not magic
Nor is it a good luck charm
It isn't meant to protect me
From every physical harm.
It's simply an understanding
Between my teammates and me.

When I put my hand in my pocket
To bring out a coin or key
The link is there to remind me
Of what a team member should be.

It links me to the team
It links me to the school
It is a constant reminder
That there is no place for a fool.

So I carry this link in my pocket
To remind me many a time
That a human without conviction
Isn't worth a simple dime.

–Norm Parker

If you must kick–kick towards the goal.

–Bob Devine

It is so easy for us to justify our own inefficiencies by criticizing others…

These things are necessary on your squad to allow the players to feel committed to the game:

- A sincere, wholesome respect for one another.

- A feeling of sensitivity by the coaches to the academic, social, etc., problems of the student athlete.

- A sincere desire to help the student athlete.

- Fairness-honesty—the players cannot feel—the reason I'm not playing is coach doesn't like me.

- Maybe the most important—there are enough people sitting around the locker room to say to the one who is always complaining—Quit your bitching and get to work!

–Dan Devine

It isn't the plays or the system that gets the job done, it's the quality of the people in the system.

–Joe Paterno

Teamwork is giving with no thought of receiving.
It's being sincere and in sincerity believing.
It's someone to talk to and someone talking to you.
It's telling and hearing what is true.
It's refusing to believe that bad exists.
It's knowing that when not around you are missed.
It's trying to help any way you can if even it's only to understand.
It's a willingness to learn how to give more.
It's getting it done without keeping score.
It's trusting in faith each and every day.
It's knowing you rate in a very special way.

There are few, if any, jobs in which *ability* alone is sufficient.
Needed also are *loyalty, sincerity, enthusiasm*, and *cooperation*.

It takes less time to do a thing *right* than it does to explain why you did it *wrong*.

The best thing to hold onto in life is each other.

Teamwork

The world is full of problems,
There's much to cause distress;
We all are bowed beneath the cares
That daily round us press.
There's only one solution,
'Tis simply stated thus:
"A little less of you or me,
A little more of us."

The rule of each one for himself
Most foolish is to follow;
It beings no savor to the game,
Its victories are hollow.
But the other plan has never failed
To bring satisfaction, plus:
"A little less of you or me,
A little more of us."

A flake of snow is very small,
'Tis lost to sight quite quickly;
But many flakes combined will fill
The roads and pathways thickly.
United we can face the fight
Without distress or fuss:
"A little less of you or me,
A little more of us."

—William T. Card

The team that makes the fewest mistakes usually wins the game.

The team that *won't* be beaten *can't* be beaten.

—Frank Broyles

Please all and you please none.

The person who rows the boat generally doesn't have time to rock it.

No person is as important as the team.

Football teams have three types of players:

- Those willing and able
- Those able and not willing
- Those willing and not able.

In order to have a winner, the team must have a feeling of unity; every player must put the team first ahead of personal glory.

—Bear Bryant

There is no "*I*" in the word team.

Every player on the team has a right to play…some more than others.

Equal opportunity for *all*, special privileges for *none*.

The amount that can be consumed and executed by a team is controlled by the weakest player on it…And while others can give that person physical help, he or she has to do his or her own thinking.

What really counts is not the number of hours you put in, but how much you put in the hours.

People with little intelligence generally are *selfish* and vice versa.

Intensity

Imagine—if you can think it, it can happen.

Noise—not by mouth, but by action.

Training—keep the team rules.

Energy—correctly applied in team effort.

Need—the great need for pride.

Sacrifice—the team comes first.

Intelligence—be smart not smart aleck.

Thoroughness—details are important.

You—are very important.

The best way to forget your own problems is to help someone else solve theirs.

We emphasize the following to each of our players:

- The importance of being on time.
- Control of temper.
- Meaning of loyalty and self-sacrifice.
- Exercising good judgment.
- Strict discipline.
- Individual responsibility.
- Sportsmanship and fair play.
- Pride in one's self and in others.
- Burning desire to excel.
- Respect of authority.

–Bron Bachevich, Roger Bacon High School,
Cincinnati, Ohio

Build for your team a *feeling of oneness*, of dependence upon one another and of strength to be derived by unity.

One of the rarest things that one ever does is the very best he or she can…

Teamwork teaches that each member of the organization must sacrifice for another— for the good of everyone.

–Frank Leahy

The real way to enjoy life is as a participant. Perhaps it's the people who think they're spectators who spread the idea that all pleasure must be paid for. Don't pay for any of it…LIFE IS FREE.

How to Be a Champion

- Exude a surplus of confidence around your competitors and self at all times, but don't be unsportsmanlike.

- Help your competitors at all times. After all, you might make a friend out of him or her.

- Study, study, study. Know your sport. Know your position.

- Question anyone you meet about her technique, how she trained, how to correct your problems. Read about successful people.

- Compete as often as possible to get experience; don't compete for medals, but for fun and companionship.

- Don't let yourself think about competing for second place; you came here to win.

- Set a concrete goal for yourself, even if you think it's impossible. Nothing is impossible for someone with faith.

- Be determined, irrespective of your size, shape, training state, equipment, or conditions.

- Always take the blame yourself for failure; study each failure with greater intensity than your success.

- Control your emotions at all times in competition, it can completely destroy your timing and coordination.

- Be critical, objective, and open-minded at all times.

- Don't drink or smoke at any time; the real champion would never do it and the others seldom do it.

- Tell your coaches what your problems seem to be and rely upon them to help you solve the difficulty.

- Study the physiology of training, the psychology of your competitors, and experiment all the time. Watch winners closely.

We may have come in *different ships*, but we're all in the *same boat* now.

The higher you go in life, the more you become dependent on others.

A group becomes a team when all members are sure enough of themselves and their contribution to praise the skills of the other.

–Norman G. Shidle

Cooperate—remember the banana—every time it leaves the bunch—it gets skinned!

The main ingredient of stardom—is the rest of the team.

Thunder is good, thunder is impressive, but it is the lightning that does the work.

–Mark Twain

New Team Rules

(Non-negotiable and applicable to all)

Rule #1: The head coach is always right.

Rule #2: If you think the head coach is wrong, refer to Rule #1.

My Recipe

I have a recipe for life,
The best one that I know:
I guarantee the end result
'Twas taught me long ago!

You start by mixing just a dash
Of humor with the day,
And then you add a cheery smile
As you go on your way.

Love's never out of season
So you add a large amount,
And I never measure sympathy—
You don't with things that count.

Toss in a bit of effort
And a lot of nerve and grit,
And hope makes all the difference,
For a thing improves with it.

You stir a bit of kindness in,
Along with patience, too,
And flavor it with gentleness
Whatever you may do.

When the sun is setting,
You'll look back in joy to see
A worthwhile product of your toil
Within my recipe!

—Grace E. Easley

The one who doesn't pull his weight is not asked to pull, while the one who does, pulls for two.

—Alexander Solzhenitsyn

"We" Makes "Me" Stronger

Geese don't get high-powered press coverage like seagulls. They're seen as dull, ordinary bulls, which only attract notice twice a year during migration.

Like the Blue Angels, they fly wingtip to wingtip. You can hear the beat of their wings whistling through the air in unison. That's the secret of their strength: together, cooperating as a flock, geese can fly a 70-percent longer range. The lead goose cuts a swath through the air resistance, which creates a helpful uplift for the two birds behind. In turn, their beating makes it easier for the birds behind them, much like the drag of a race car sucked in behind the lead car. Each bird takes his or her turn at being the leader. The tired ones fan out to the edges of the "V" for a breather, and the rested ones surge toward the point of the "V" to drive the flock onward.

If a goose becomes too exhausted or ill and has to drop out of the flock, he or she is never abandoned. A stronger member of the flock will follow the failing, weak one to his or her resting place and wait until he or she is well enough to fly again. They will then join up with another flock.

Don't

If an impulse comes to say some thoughtless word today that may drive a friend away, don't say it.

If you've heard a word of blame cast upon your neighbors' name that may injure their fair fame, don't tell it.

If malicious gossip's tongue some vile slander may have flung on the head of old or young, don't repeat it.

Even if the story is true, think of all the harm it would do: How much better, then, if you don't rehearse it.

Thoughtful, kind, helpful speech, 'tis a gift vouchsafed to each, this is the lesson we would teach: don't abuse it.

The Team

All championship teams always possess the most important factor of success: great team unity! Championship coaches and players on why their teams won championships:

Some say you have to use your five best players, but I found out you win with the five that fit together best as a team.

–Red Auerbach, former coach of the Boston Celtics,
won eight straight national titles

The only way to win is to sacrifice for the good of the team.

–Bill Sharman, coached ABA and NBA teams to championships

It's simple: the best team always wins.

–Bill Russell, played on 11 NBA championship teams in 13 years,
and led the Celtics to the championships two of the three years he coached

The Packers won the Super Bowl primarily because the team had a lot of love for each other and this unity helped us hold up under pressure.

–Vince Lombardi, legendary professional football coach

Our titles would not have been possible without the unselfishness displayed by all our teams: the team wins, not the individuals.

–John Wooden, greatest coach in the history of basketball

This is a team game and one man doesn't win. In the end the best team usually wins.

–Wilt Chamberlain, greatest offensive player in basketball and member of two NBA championship teams, holds NBA record for most points in a game

Loyalty is faithfulness, effort, and enthusiasm. It is common decency plus common sense. Loyalty is making yourself part of an organization and making it part of you.

–from Good Reading

We are all equal in that we are all different.

There is no team on our schedule that we cannot beat. There is no team on the schedule that cannot beat us. What then is the answer? 1. Physical Readiness, 2. Mental Readiness, 3. A readiness of football knowledge. Let us take a moment and look at each.

1. Physical Readiness: I feel that, for those of you who participated, we got a good start in that direction this spring; you must take over this summer and continue what we are doing. We will send a workout sheet that will give you a guide to go by. The tempo of your program must build up to August, and we expect that each of you will report ready to go two-a-day. If we must spend time getting you ready physically, we will lose valuable time on the technique and teamwork that we need to beat Colorado. Don't sabotage yourself and your team by reporting out of shape.

2. Mental Readiness: This is pretty much your problem. The coaching staff will do all they can to motivate your efforts, but basically, you must want to play, and want to win for the SPARTANS. There are many times when it will take moral fiber and great courage to continue, but we must continue. Start now to prepare yourself for a great season. Let's dedicate ourselves to the task, and the challenge that lies ahead. It will take a man to do the job. I hope we have many who qualify.

3. Readiness of Football Knowledge: This is a joint problem; we will supply you with a great deal of material. We expect you to read it and to learn it. How well you do this will play a major role in how well you do and how well the team does.

There you have it: 1-2-3. It will take all three to win. It will take a man of character to excel in all three. It will take a team that excels in all three to win.

—Norm Parker, MSU Summer letter

The best players help others to be best players.

There's something very democratic about baseball box scores—they don't tell how big you are, or what your religion is, or what your father or mother was. They only tell how good you were on a particular day. Somewhere there's a person keeping score on everything you do and on every move you make, good or bad. You can fool yourself, but you can't fool the figures. The game statistics tell what you did that particular day. They don't ask many questions, but they hold most of the answers.

Athletic Participation

- Provides an opportunity to develop your physical powers to the fullest.

- Develops responsiveness to group discipline.

- Develops lasting friendships.

- Develops self-confidence.

- Develops respect for rules and duly constituted authority.

- Gives opportunities for development of cooperation, resourcefulness, gameness, initiative, and unselfishness.

- Enables you to see other communities and get acquainted with others through travel.

- May help you through college.

The Call of the Wild

You're sick of the game, why, that's a shame; you're young, you're brave and you're bright. You have had a raw deal, I know, but don't squeal, buck up! Do your darndest and fight! It's the plugging away that will win you the day. So don't be a piker 'ole pard; just call on your grit, it's so easy to quit. It's keeping on living that's hard.

It's easy to cry that you're beaten, and die. It's easy to crawfish and crawl, but to fight and to fight when hope's out of sight, why, that's the best game of them all. And although you come out of each grueling bout all broken and beaten and scarred, just give one more try; it's so easy to die. It's keeping your chin up that's hard.

—Robert Service

A genius is one who shoots at something no one else can see, and hits it.

A good friend never gets in your way unless you're on your way down.

Communicate

Clear—Be understood while talking and writing.

Organized—Pre-plan order of taking and giving information.

Meaningful—Conversations.

Measures—Keep accurate records.

Unity—Work together.

Notes—Write information down; use notes for reference.

Information—Not emotions.

Concise—Say what you mean in as few words as possible.

Accuracy—Only the fact is no guesswork.

Time—Do not waste it.

Expect the unexpected—Have alternate plans ready if something goes wrong.

Teamwork

It's all very well to have courage and skill and it's fine to be counted a star. But the single deed with its touch of thrill does not tell the players you are: For there is no lone hand in the game we play, we must work to a bigger scheme. And the thing that counts in the world today is "How do you pull with the team?"

They may sound our praise and call you great, they may single you out for fame. But you must work with your running mate or you'll never win the game: Oh, never the work of life is done by the one with a selfish dream, for the battle is lost or the battle is won by the spirit of the team.

You may think it fine to be praised for skill, but a greater thing to do is to set your mind and set your will on the goal that's just in view: It is helping your fellow players to score when their chances hopeless seem: It is forgetting self 'til the game is over and fighting for the team.

—Edgar A. Guest

A friend is one who walks in when the others walk out.

A head coach is guided by this main objective: dig, claw, wheedle, coax that fanatical effort out of the players. You want your team to play on Saturday as if they were planting the flag on Iwo Jima.

–Darrell Royal

Friends are what you think you have plenty of until you need just one.

Most athletes are willing to change, not because they see the light, but because they feel the heat.

No problem can stand the assault of sustained thinking.

9

Winning

❖

Success

The hardest thing about climbing the Ladder of Success is getting through the crowd at the bottom.

Success and sacrifice are brothers.

Photo: Shaun Botterill/Getty Images

I will persist until I succeed.

I was not delivered into this world in defeat, nor does failure course in my veins.

I am not a sheep waiting to be prodded by my shepherd.

I am a winner and I refuse to talk or walk with sheep.

The slaughterhouse of failure is not my destiny.

I will persist until I succeed.

The big game of next week, month, or year is being won or lost right now!

Winning is important. *Winning* has a joy and discrete purity that cannot be replaced by anything else. *Winning* is important to everyone's sense of satisfaction and well-being. It is not everything, but it is something powerful, indeed beautiful, in itself—something as essential to the spirit as striving is to the character.

—A Bartlett Giamatti, President, Yale University

True success is the only thing that you cannot have unless and until you have offered it to others.

Napoleon once observed, "An army's effectiveness depends on its size, training, experience, and morale. And morale is worth more than all the other factors combined."

Make up your mind to act decidedly and take the consequences. No good is ever done in this world by hesitation.

—Thomas Henry Huxley

What is the Price of Success?

To use all of your courage to force yourself to concentrate on the problem at hand, to think of it deeply and constantly, to study it from all angles and to plan.

To have a high and sustained determination to put over what you play to accomplish, not if circumstances be favorable to its accomplishment, but in spite of all adverse circumstances, which may arise…and nothing worthwhile has ever been accomplished without some obstacles to overcome.

To refuse to believe that there are any circumstances sufficiently strong to defeat you in the accomplishment of your purpose.

The Rules for Success

- Find your own particular talent.
- Be big.
- Be honest.
- Live with enthusiasm.
- Don't let your possessions possess you.
- Don't worry about your problems.
- Look up to people when you can—down to no one.
- Don't cling to the past.
- Assume your full share of responsibility in the world.
- Strive to be happy.

Successful individuals make up their minds what they want and then go after it with everything in them.

The will to win is worthless if you do not have the will to prepare.

One who has heart has hope, and one who has hope has everything.

—Arabian proverb

Success without honor is an unseasoned dish; it will satisfy your hunger, but it won't taste good.

—Joe Paterno

We are what we repeatedly do…Excellence, then, is not an act but a habit.

—Aristotle

The dictionary is the only place *success* comes before *work*.

Success

Success is speaking words of praise
In cheering other people's ways,
In doing just the best you can
With every task and every plan.
It's silence when your speech would hurt.
Politeness when your neighbor's curt.
It's deafness when the scandal flows,
And sympathy with other's woes.
It's loyalty when duty calls,
It's courage when disaster falls,
It's patience when the hours are long;
It's found in laughter and in song;
It's in the silent time of prayer,
In happiness and in despair
In all of life and nothing less
We find the thing we call success.

Success is getting what you want; happiness is wanting what you get.

I don't like to lose, and that isn't so much because it is just a football game, but because the defeat means the failure to reach your objective. The trouble in American life today, in business as well as in sports, is that too many people are afraid of competition. The result is that in some circles people have come to sneer at success if it costs hard work and training and sacrifice.

–Knute Rockne

Pride is the basis of winning football.

–Darryl Royal

It's great to be great, but it's greater to be human.

–Will Rogers

It ain't braggin' if you've done it.

If you have tried to do something and *failed*, you are vastly better off than if you had tried to do nothing and *succeeded*.

Once you've won or lost, it's behind you. What lies ahead is all that matters.

–Bud Wilkinson

Keep A-Goin'

Do your darnest when you play,
Keep a-goin'.
To take it easy doesn't pay,
Keep a-goin'.
When the game is pretty tough,
Don't you ever holler "nuff,"
Show the world you have the stuff,
Keep a-goin'.
You only need a harder punch,
Keep a-goin'.
'Tain't no use to stand and whine
When they're coming through your line;
Hitch your trousers up and climb,
Keep a-goin'.
If the other team's on top,
Keep a-goin'.
That's just the time you must not stop,
Keep a-goin'.
'S'pose they stop 'most every play;
One good long run may win the day;
To get discouraged doesn't pay,
Keep a-goin'.
When it seems the game is lost,
Keep a-goin'.
Do not stop at any cost—
Keep a-goin'.
Don't ever think that you can't win it,
A fightin' team is always in it;
So don't let up a single minute,
Keep a-goin'.

The royal road to success would have more travelers if so many weren't lost attempting to find shortcuts.

—H. C. Calvin

The Optimist vs. the Pessimist

The optimist turns the impossible into the possible; the pessimist turns the possible into the impossible.

The optimist pleasantly ponders how high the kite will fly; the pessimist woefully wonders how soon the kite will fall.

The optimist sees a green near every sand trap; the pessimist sees a sand trap near every green.

The optimist looks at the horizon and sees an opportunity; the pessimist peers into the distance and fears a problem.

To the optimist all doors have handles and hinges; to the pessimist all doors have locks and latches.

The optimist promotes progress, prosperity, and plenty; the pessimist preaches limitations, liabilities, and losses.

The optimist accentuates assets, abundance, and advantages; the pessimist majors in mistakes, misfortunes, and misery.

The optimist goes out and finds the bell; the pessimist gives up and wrings his or her hands.

–William Arthur Ward

A successful person is one who went ahead and did the thing the rest of us never quite got around to.

Success is not a harbor but a voyage with its own perils to the spirit.

–Richard Huger

When your arms are so tired that you can hardly lift your hands to come on guard, *fight one more round*. When your nose is bleeding and your eyes are black and you are so tired that you wish your opponent would crack you one in the jaw and put you to sleep, *fight one more round*—remembering that the one who always fights one more round is never whipped.

–James J. Corbell, heavyweight champ

The final goal is winning…anything that distracts from winning must be done away with.

–George Perles

A winning habit is like a cable…a thread is woven each day until the product becomes unbreakable.

The difference between *champ* and *chump* is "U".

57 Rules for Success

First, deliver the goods.

Second, the other 56 don't matter.

Words are leaves—Deeds are fruit.

It is impossible to get a toehold on success by acting like a heel.

The path to success is never a five lane, no traffic, superhighway. Heartbreak, setbacks, frustrations, failures, enemies…appear time and again to prevent you from reaching your goals.

—N. C. Stone

Your ship won't come in till you row out to meet it.

In any test of skills we either get better or we slip backward. Start where you are with what you have; and make something better of it.

The kiss system of teaching: Keep it simple stupid.

Winners never quit, and quitters never win.

It is easier to become a champion than to stay a champion.

Treat people nicely on the way up, you're liable to meet them again on the way down.

Practice does not make perfect.
Perfect practice makes perfect.

The Only Way to Win

It takes a little courage
And a little self-control,
And some grim determination,
If you want to reach your goal.
It takes a deal of striving,
And a firm and stern-set chin,
No matter what the battle,
If you really want to win.

There's no easy path to glory,
There's no rosy road to fame.
Life, however we may view it,
Is no simple parlor game;
But its prizes call for fighting,
For endurance and for grit;
For a rugged disposition
And a don't-know-when-to-quit.

You must take a blow or give one,
You must risk and you must lose,
And expect that in the struggle,
You will suffer from the bruise,
But you mustn't wince or falter,
If a fight you once begin;
Be an athlete, face the battle—
That's the only way to win.

The wind blows the strongest upon those who stand the tallest.

—F. C. Hayes

Success consists of doing the common things uncommonly well.

Buck Nystrom's Four Corners of Success

Commitment		Effort
	Success	
Motivation		Discipline

Inside inefficiency is more to be feared than outside competition.

Every successful person I have heard of has done the best he could with the conditions as he found them, and not waited until next year for better.

–E. W. Howe

Thoughts of a Winner

Although I am only one out of a million, I am somebody, and that makes me as good as the next person.

There is nothing in this life I cannot do. There is no goal I cannot tackle and have success! If I feel deep down inside that something is important to me, then I can do it. If my mind can conceive it, and my head can believe it, then I know I can achieve it. No longer will I drift through life feeling sorry for myself, because self-pity is the seed of destruction.

I will search for a goal, and with enough hard work, total commitment, determination, dedication, and self-sacrifice, I know I will reach it. I know there will be many times when it will seem that all the odds are against me, and I will have to fight one battle after another—but I will not give up!

Success...

Success is the way you walk the paths of life each day.
It's in the little things you do, and in the things you say.
It's not in reaching heights or fame, it's not, alone,
  in reaching goals, that all humans seek to claim.
Success is being big of heart and clean and broad of mind.
Success is being faithful to your friends, and to the stranger, kind.
Success is in the team, the coaches, and the family that you love,
  and what they learn from you.
Success is having character, in everything you do.

Chance favors the prepared mind.

–Louis Pasteur

It is one thing to *itch* for something and another to *scratch* for it.

The race is not always to the swift but most often to the one who keeps on running.

Time cannot be purchased, marketed, or saved. It can only be *spent*. The secret, then, is to spend it *wisely*.

If at first you don't succeed, you're doing about average.

Motivation is what gets you started. Habit is what keeps you going.

–Jim Ryun

It Takes Only Two Percent

Have you been working like a horse? I've been thinking about that expression—and at least one horse I can name has earned a pretty fair hourly rate. Someone has figured out that the race horse, Nashua, earned more than a million dollars in a total racing time that added up to less than one hour!

That's pretty good pay. Of course, we know that many, many more hours went into preparing for that winning hour of racing.

But there is something else here that interests me. What is there about a horse like Nashua that made him such a consistent winner and made him so valuable? You'd probably pay a hundred times as much for a horse like Nashua as you would for an ordinary racehorse. But is he a hundred times faster? No. To be a consistent winner and to be worth a hundred times as much as the average, he needed only to be consistent in finishing just ahead of the rest.

All he had to do was win a good share of the time by a nose to be worth a hundred times as much as an also-ran. And so it is with human beings who are on top in the game of life.

A writer in a national magazine made the assertion that the difference between the individual of achievement and that individual of mediocrity is a difference of only about two percent in study, application, interest, attention, and effort. Only about two percent separates the winner from the loser!

A boxer can win the world's championship simply by winning one more round than his opponent—or even by being only a point or two ahead. And this narrow margin can make the difference between fame and fortune or never being heard of again! It's often a matter of only two percent. We have no idea of what a change we could make in our results if we would simply add that two percent more time and effort than the average person is willing to put in.

—Gene Emmet Clark, D.D.

It is better to have faith in a cause that will ultimately succeed, than to succeed in a cause that will ultimately fail.

Some say the will to win is a bad thing. In what way? Education is supposed to prepare a student for life, and life is competition. Success in life goes only to the person who competes and wins. A successful lawyer is the one who goes out and wins—wins law cases. A successful physician is a doctor who goes out and wins—saves lives and restores patients to health. A successful sales manager is a person who goes out and wins—sells the goods. The successful executive is the one who can make money. There is no reward for losing. So that leaves living life only one way—with the will to win.

—Knute Rockne

Success Formula for Coaching and for Life

Work + Discipline + Pride + Team = Success + Winning

Work—In the quest of success in life's endeavors work is essential. Give yourself, 100%, to whatever you are attempting.

Discipline—We must discipline ourselves to avoid the mistakes that hinder our development.

Pride—Once we possess a sense of work and discipline, pride is developed in ourselves and we know we are the best at what we do.

Team—Very few things are done individually. The majority of our accomplishments are done as a team. This is certainly true in athletics and it also holds true for the business world, the Church, and other institutions in our society.

Success—The combination of the above four equate to success. The degree of success we achieve depends on how well we've mastered the work, discipline, pride, and team concepts. If the degree of success continues to be small, then one or more of the four concepts needs to be re-evaluated and improved.

Winning—Winning in athletics and in life is merely a by-product of this success formula. If you continue to develop these attributes, winning will come to you.

—Tom Stobie

No coach or teacher ever won a game by what he or she knows: It is what his or her players have learned that wins.

Seventeen Secrets to Success...

1. Keep your temper to yourself
2. Give your enthusiasm to everybody
3. Be yourself, but become genuinely interested in the other guy
4. Be fair, honest, and friendly and you'll be admired and liked
5. Make others feel important
6. Count your assets and stamp our self-pity
7. Meet the other person at his/her own level
8. Put your smile power to work
9. Keep moving
10. Keep trying
11. Give the gift of heart
12. Get off to a good start in anything you do
13. Forgive yourself if you fail
14. Be lavish with kindness
15. Overwhelm people with your charm, not power
16. Keep your promises
17. Be an optimist

Always remember that there is a law of compensation which operates just as infallibly as gravitation, and that victory goes at last where it ought to, and that this is just as true of individuals as it is of nations.

–William Feather

The Will to Win

If you want a thing bad enough to go out and fight for it, give up your time and your peace and your sleep for it, if only the desire of it makes you quite mad enough never to tire, makes you perceive all other things tawdry and cheap for it, if life seems empty and useless without it and all that you scheme and you dream is about it...

If gladly you'll sweat for it, fret for it, lose all your terror of God or of man for it, if you'll simply go after that thing that you want, with all your capacity, strength and sagacity, faith, hope and confidence, stern pertinacity, if neither cold poverty, famish and gaunt, nor sickness nor pain of body and brain can turn you away from the thing that you want, if dogged and grim you besiege and beset it... you'll get it.

–Berton Braley

Coaching Points

- Coaching is the same on all levels. The basic ingredient is communication. You have to teach, communicate, and demand. You get out of people what you demand from them.

- What you teach differs on each level. The "How" on the lower levels and the "What" on the Pro level.

- On the professional level you have to be a better communicator. You are dealing with a more sophisticated person. In all cases you have to consider individual differences.

- I became a better coach when I quit worrying about my next job. Don't become too involved in a mass of details (Paralysis through analysis).

- Surround yourself with a good staff. Instill within them the need to do a better job than anyone else ever did in their specific responsibility.

- Confidence means that you know you prepared harder than anyone else.

Progress is not created by contented people.

–Frank Tyger

You Can Start Here

"What is this place noted for?" asked a traveler of an old-time resident. "Why, mister, this is the starting point for any place in the world. You can start here and go anywhere you want to."

How true! Yet how many of us fail to realize the full richness of living because we always yearn to be somewhere else before starting seriously on our journey to the place we wish to be. Someone should write a book about the lives that have been impoverished spiritually and materially because of the "if" which enters into most major decisions we must make—the "if" which prevents us from starting where we are and striking out directly for the goal of our hopes. It is impossible to start form some other place—we must begin where we are, using what we have, and launch out upon our journey.

This is the starting point for anyplace in the world. Look under your own doorsteps to find the material you need. Then, on your mark, get set, and go!

–Leo Bennett

Everyday Success Pointers...

- Can't means won't try.
- Your mind is the place where all progress begins and ends.
- To every difficulty, there is a solution.
- To discover a weakness is the beginning of strength.
- Your goal becomes your potential worth.
- Whatever you focus your attention upon, you give strength to.
- Nothing is impossible for a willing mind.
- Genius is to take the complicated and make it simple.
- We can change our lives by merely changing our attitudes.
- To lose your fighting spirit is to lose all.
- If you meet someone without a smile give them yours, it costs nothing but will pay rich dividends.
- Some people make things happen, some wait for things to happen, and then there are those who say what happened!

Cripple him, and you have a Sir Walter Scott.

Lock him in a prison cell, and you have a John Bunyan.

Bury him in snows of Valley Forge, and you have a George Washington.

Raise him in abject poverty, and you have Abraham Lincoln.

Subject him to bitter religious prejudice, and you have a Disraeli.

Afflict him with asthma as a child, and you have a Theodore Roosevelt.

Stop him with rheumatic pains until he can't sleep without an opiate, and you have a Steinmetz.

Put him in a grease pit of a locomotive roundhouse, and you have a Toscanini.

Spit on him, humiliate him, then crucify him and he forgives you, and you have Jesus Christ.

Strike him down with infantile paralysis, and he becomes FDR.

When he is a lad of eight, burn him so severely in a schoolhouse fire that the doctors say he will never walk again, and you have a Glen Cunningham.

Deafen a genius composer and you have a Ludwig bon Beethoven (who continued to compose some of the world's most beautiful music).

Drag him, more dead than alive, out of a rice paddy in Vietnam, and you have a Rocky Bleier.

Have him or her born black in a society filled with racial discrimination, and you have Booker T. Washington, Harriet Tubman, or Martin Luther King Jr., Marion Anderson, and George Washington Carver.

Call a slow learner "retarded" and write him off as uneducable, and you have an Albert Einstein.

All young people ambitious to succeed must first cultivate willpower, for without willpower they will never triumph over all the obstacles and difficulties they are sure to encounter in the pursuit of their goal. Real success is akin to willpower in that it lies in the mind, the heart, the soul, a thing oftentimes invisible to the eye of others. Our future and our fate lie in our wills more than in our hands, for our hands are but the instruments of our wills.

–B. C. Forbes

Overcoming obstacles, getting torn up inside, then winning—that's what life and football is all about.

–George Allen

To sin by silence when they should protest makes cowards out of humans.

–Abraham Lincoln

Civilization is always in danger when those who have never learned to obey are given the right to command.

–Fulton Sheen

The world hates change; yet it is the only thing that has brought progress.

Not in the clamor of the crowded streets, not in the shouts and plaudits of the throng, but within ourselves are victory and defeat.

Leadership is a matter of having people look at you and gain confidence, seeing how you react. If you're in control, they're in control.

–Tom Landry

Many of us don't have to turn out the lights to be in the dark.

Happiness is doing—not having.

The Winners

They only win who reach the gate
Through surf and storm and bitter gale,
Through pain and loneliness and hate,
Through all the sullen thrusts of fate,
With battered prow and tattered sail,
Who look on life and death as one,
Until the closing race is run.

Those only win who see the goal,
Beyond the baffling fog and mist,
Whose names are written on the scroll
Of those who stand with unbowed soul
Soul amid the thin, immortal list
Who drive through fear amid the thin
Until the darkness closes in.

This is no life for soul or heart
That breaks or falters at defeat:
The weak are beaten at the start,
And only those who play their part
May face the rough and rocky beat:
The road is long, the dream is gone
Yet the fighting heart still carries on.

—Grantland Rice

Wise men and women in every culture have maintained that the secret of happiness is not in getting more but in wanting less.

—Philip Slater

The trouble with success is that the formula is the same as the one for a nervous breakdown.

—*Executives' Digest*

A successful person is one who has tried, not cried; who has worked, not dodged; who has shouldered responsibility, not evaded it; who has lifted the burden instead of standing off, looking on, and giving advice.

–Elbert Hubbard

What sets off a champion from his adversities in any activity is his ability to combine the maximum of concentration with the optimum of relaxation, so that he is fully alert but never tense.

–Sidney J. Harris

Success

Success isn't never making mistakes: It's never giving up when I make mistakes.

Success isn't always accomplishing everything I set out to do: It's always setting out to do what I know I can accomplish.

Success isn't always knowing how to say what I feel: It's always knowing how to feel what I say.

Success isn't being a perfect person: It's being glad I am not perfect so I can understand others.

Success isn't what people think I am: It's what I am.

Success isn't being the superstar who always gets the applause: It's sitting back and letting someone else get the credit.

Success isn't supporting myself with superficial achievements: It's finding myself submerged in the process of God's eternal success.

–Ken Harris

Ten Commandments of Success

1. Work Hard. Hard work is the best investment a person can make.

2. Study Hard. Knowledge enables a person to work more intelligently and effectively.

3. Have Initiative. Ruts often deepen into graves.

4. Love Your Work. Then you will find pleasure in mastering it.

5. Be Exact. Slipshod methods bring slipshod results.

6. Have the Spirit of Conquest. Thus you can successfully battle and overcome difficulties.

7. Cultivate Personality. Personality is to a human what perfume is to the flower.

8. Help and Share with Others. The real test of business greatness lies in giving opportunity to others.

9. Be Democratic. Unless you feel right towards your fellow beings you can never be a successful leader.

10. In All Things Do Your Best. The one who has done his or her best has done everything. The one who has done less than his or her best has done nothing.

–Charles M. Schwab

Some people are so indecisive, their favorite color is plaid.

The sense of success is to set a long-range goal and be able to relate daily work to it. Too many of us have only a vague idea of what we ultimately want. Even if we do, we may not know how to translate this desire into the necessary short-range steps that will get us there.

The person who is not afraid of failure seldom has to face it.

If at first you do succeed, try something harder.

10

Work

❖

Education

Good luck often has the odor of perspiration about it.

He who is only an athlete is too crude, too vulgar, too much a savage. He who is a scholar only is too soft, too effeminate. The ideal citizen is the scholar-athlete.

–Plato

Photo: Lara Jo Regan/Getty Images

Ways to Excel on the Job

If you want to save your job and move up the ladder, apply some of these suggestions offered by Professor Paul Timm of Brigham Young University:

- Do it now. Immediate follow-up impresses bosses.

- Learn to exceed your employer's expectations. Be more than satisfactory. Do the job faster or better than you did before.

- Know what your boss wants. Meet periodically with your supervisor or manager to make sure you're giving assignments the proper emphasis and you're not neglecting important assignments.

- Get good at what you do. Seek areas where your special skills and interests are best used. Become so good that it would be difficult to accomplish certain things without you.

- Be as positive as possible. People like to work with others who are optimistic and cheerful. Encourage people around you.

- Invest in yourself. Keep growing. Attend professional meetings. Participate in training opportunities and take courses to acquire skills and make contacts.

- Invest in planning your day, week, year, and career. Use a daily planner and spend time with it each day. When you plan, decide what you're going to do and what results you expect.

Source: *51 Ways to Save Your Job,* by Paul Timm

Submit to pressure from peers and you move down to their level.

Speak up for your own beliefs and you invite them up to your level.

If you move with the crowd, you'll get no further than the crowd.

When 40 million people believe in a dumb idea, it's still a dumb idea.

Simply swimming with the tide leaves you nowhere.

So if you believe in something that's good, honest, and bright, stand up for it.

Maybe your peers will get smart and drift your way.

–United Technologies

Keep On Keepin' On

If the day looks kinder gloomy and your chances kinder slim, and the situation's puzzlin', and the prospect awful grim, and perplexities keep a-pressin' till all hope is nearly gone—Just bristle up and grit your teeth and keep on keepin' on.

Fumin' never wins a fight, and frettin' never pays.
There ain't no good in broodin' in those pessimistic ways; smile just kinder cheerfully when hope is nearly gone, and bristle up and grit your teeth and keep on keepin' on.

There ain't no use in growlin' and grumblin' all the time, when the music's ringin' everywhere, and everything's in rhyme.
Just keep on smilin' cheerfully if hope is nearly gone, and bristle up and grit your teeth and keep on keepin' on.

One Iota More

The thing that makes a champion is obvious enough:
It isn't any mystic prestidigitator's stuff.
It's nothing more than giving to whatever be the chore
The power is in you—and a small scintilla more.

It isn't any wizardry, it's not a magic gift,
It's merely lifting honestly the load you have to lift,
Or, in the game you're playing, it is using all your store of grit and nerve and energy—
    and just a trifle more.

The thing that makes a champion is simple, plain, and clear; it's never being
    "almost," "just about," or "pretty near."
It's summoning the utmost from your spirit's inner core and giving every bit of it—and
    just a little more.

"That little more—how much it is." As deep and wide and far as that enormous
    emptiness from molehill to a star,
The gulf between the earthbound and the eagles as they soar,
The champions give their best—and one iota more.

Dear Teacher:

My young child starts to school today…it's all going to be strange and new for a while, I hope you will be gentle. You see, up to now, he's been king of the roost…he's been boss of the backyard…his mother has always been around to repair his wounds, and I've always been handy to soothe his feelings. But now things are going to be different.

This morning he's going to walk down the front steps, wave his hand, and start out on the great adventure…it's an adventure that might take him across continents. It's an adventure that will probably include wars and tragedy and sorrow. To live his life in the world he has to live in will require faith and love and courage.

So, World, I wish you would sort of take him by his young hand and teach him the things he will have to know. Teach him, but gently, if you can.

What He Must Learn

He will have to learn, I know that all men are not just, that all men are not true.

But teach him also that for every scoundrel there is a hero; that for every crooked politician there is a dedicated leader; teach him that for every enemy, there is a friend.

It will take time, World, I know, but teach him, if you can, that a nickel earned is of far more value than a dollar found; teach him to learn to lose and to enjoy winning.

Steer him away from envy, if you can, and teach him the secret of quiet laughter.

The world stands aside to let anyone pass who knows where he is going.

—Jordan

No athlete will work for your interests unless they are hers.

Let him learn early that the bullies are the easiest people to lick; teach him, if you can, the wonder of books, but also give him quiet time to ponder the eternal mystery of birds in the sky and flowers on a green hill.

In school, World, teach him it is far more honorable to fail than to cheat; teach him to have faith in his own ideas, even if everyone tells him they are wrong; teach him to be gentle with gentle people and tough with tough people.

Not to Follow the Crowd

Try to give my child the strength not to follow the crowd when everyone else is getting on the bandwagon; teach him to listen to all men, but teach him also to filter all he hears on a screen of truth and take only the good that comes through.

Teach him, if you can, how to laugh when he is sad; teach him there is no shame in tears; teach him there can be glory in failure and despair in success.

Teach him to scoff at cynics and to beware of too much sweetness; teach him to sell his brawn and brains to the highest bidders but never to put a price tag on his heart and soul.

Teach him to close his ears to a howling mob; and teach him to stand and fight if he thinks he's right.

Treat him gently, World, but don't coddle him, because only the test of fire makes fine steel; let him have the courage to be impatient; let him have the patience to be brave.

Teach him always to have sublime faith in himself, because then he will always have sublime faith in mankind. This is a big order, World, but see what you can do. He's such a nice little fellow, my son!

The American College testing Service (ACT) study showed that the only factor that could be used in predicting success in later life was achievement in extracurricular activities. Grades in high school and college and ACT scores are not factors.

Even a mosquito doesn't get a slap on the back until he or she starts to work.

Let Something Good Be Said

When over the fair flame of friend or foe,
The shadow of disgrace shall fall; instead
Of words of blame, or proof of so and so,
Let something good be said.

Forget not that no fellow-being yet
May fall so low but love may lift his head;
Even the check of shame with tears is wet,
If something good be said.

No generous heart may vainly turn aside
In ways of sympathy; no soul so dead
But may awaken strong and glorified,
If something good be said.

And so I charge ye, by the thorny crown,
And by the cross on which the Savior bled,
And by your own soul's hope for fair renown,
Let something good be said.

—James W. Riley

Nine Ways To Change People Without Giving Offense or Arousing Resentment

1. Begin with praise and honest appreciation.
2. Call attention to people's mistakes indirectly.
3. Talk about your own mistakes before criticizing the other person.
4. Ask questions instead of giving orders.
5. Let the other person save face.
6. Praise the slightest improvement and praise every improvement. Be hearty in your approbation and lavish in your praise.
7. Give the other person a fine reputation to live up to.
8. Use encouragement. Make the fault seem easy to correct.
9. Make the other person happy about doing the thing you suggest.

You can't turn back the clock.
But you can wind it up again.

People are always blaming their circumstances for what they are. I don't believe in circumstances. The people who GET ON in this world are the people who GET UP and look for the circumstances they want, and, if they can't find them, MAKE THEM.

–George Bernard Shaw

Are you playing the game on the field of life?
Are you keeping within the rules?
Do you play with a jump and a joy in the strife,
Nor whimper for better tools?

There is always a chap who lags behind,
And wails that the world is gray;
That his ax is dull, and his wheel won't grind,
And it's too late to begin today.

But if you should ask the other chap,
The one who has gone ahead,
You'll find that his tools were worse, mayhap;
And he's made new ones instead.

For playing the game means not to grin,
When the field is smooth and clear;
But to fight from the first for the joy therein,
Nor to heed the haunt of fear.

And though in the strife no prize you earn
That marks the victor's fame;
Know still, if you've tried at every turn,
You have won, for you've played the game!

–Raymond Comstock

Why Are You Tired?...

We have some absolutely irrefutable statistics that show why you are tired, and it's no wonder you are tired. There aren't as many people working as you may have thought—at least according to this survey.

The population of this country is 200 million, but there are 62 million over 80 years of age. That leaves 138 million to do the work. People under 21 total 94 million—that leaves 44 million to do the work. Then there are 21 million who are employed by the government, which leaves 23 million to do the work. 10 million are in the armed forces, which leaves 13 million to do the work. There are 12,800,000 in the state and city offices, leaving 200,000 to do the work. There are 126,000 in hospitals, etc., so that leaves 74,000 to do the work. However, 62,000 bums or vagrants refuse to work so that leaves 12,000. 11,998 are in jail, which leaves 2 people to do the work—that's you and me, and I'm getting tired of doing everything myself.

Duties delayed are the devil's delight.

Make a good rule, and pray to God to help you to keep it. Never, if possible, lie down at night without being able to say: I have made one human being, at least, a little wiser, a little happier, or a little better this day.

–Charles Kingsley

Ingenuity, plus courage, plus work equals miracles.

–Rev. Bob Richards

When you affirm big, believe big, and pray big, big things happen.

–Norman Vincent Peale

Which Are You?

A little more kindness
A little less speed,
A little more giving,
A little less greed,
A little more smile,
A little less frown,
A little less kicking,
A man while he's down,
A little more "We,"
A little less "I,"
A little more laugh,
A little less cry,
A little more flowers
On the pathway of life,
And fewer on graves
At the end of the strife.

The trouble with the world is not that people know too little, but that they know so many things that ain't so.

–Mark Twain

Opportunity

They do me wrong who say I come no more when once I knock and fail to find you in; For every day I stand outside your door, and bid you wake, and rise to fight and win.

Wail not for precious chances passed away, wail not for golden ages on the wane! Each night I burn the records of that day; and at sunrise every soul is born again.

–Walter Malone

Your interest should be in the future because you're going to spend the rest of your life there.

A Boy's Idols

When I was six years old, I idolized two boys older than I by five and seven years. Both had all the makings of fine athletes. I watched them constantly as they caught a pass, hit a baseball, made a basket and I pictured the day when I would be like them.

It thrilled me to catch a pass thrown by them, a ball pitched by them, or retrieve a basketball shot by them. My day was made when they would say "hello" or simply nod their head in my direction. They were my idols. I longed to be an athlete just like them.

I grew and they grew.

I watched and listened as they bragged about cheating in school. I absorbed all of the ways of cribbing on exams. The hidden answers written on the palm of the hand, the half-opened book on the floor.

I listened as they told of how they took it easy in practice sessions; how they refused to block for a teammate they didn't like; how they chewed Dentyne and rubbed their hands with after-shave lotion so the coach wouldn't know they were smoking.

I listened as they bragged about how many beers they could drink; how many girls they had had; how many nights they had broken curfew.

I listened as they called their mother "old lady" and their father "old man," as they called this teacher and that coach something else. I listened as they spoke of Church and God being non-existent. I listened as they bragged about telling off a teacher; about stealing library books; about stealing equipment from the locker room.

I listened as they laughed about quitting a team; being thrown off a team; being thrown out of a game for fighting; being thrown out of school.

I listened as they swore. Man, they were the greatest! They were my idols. I longed to be an athlete just like them.

A lot of people love their jobs. It's the work they hate.

I grew and they grew.

I became a man. Suddenly, I saw my life in perspective. I wondered about my two idols. Surely they were successful; surely they were All-Americans; surely they were pillars of their community.

I searched and I found them. Alas, both had given up struggling to establish themselves as plain, ordinary people. They had set no records; achieved no goals; set no world on fire.

Once I had worshipped them. Now, no one in the community gave them a second look.

Then I wondered; could some young, aspiring athlete have idolized me? Had I led him down the same trail I had followed; had he longed to be an athlete—just like me?

My parents: could I ever repay them for the sorrow and anguish I had brought them? My teachers and coaches: could I ever befriend them? Other people had suffered because of me; could they ever forgive me? That young aspiring athlete; could he forgive me? Where is he now?

They have grown older and so have I.

Now I am a parent. I love my sons deeply. I want them to love God. I want them to serve man. I want them to be athletes.

My sons will watch and listen to you because you are athletes. You will wear the Green and White. Many other sons will watch and listen to you, too. You are their idols. They will long to be athletes just like you. You will grow and they will grow.

Someday you may have sons. Perhaps my sons will be their idols. Your sons will want to be just like them.

–Stu Brynn, Football Coach, Tabor College (Hillsboro, Kansas)

To get the true measure of an individual, note how much more she does than is required of her.

The Big Game

You take the color and the flash of the game,
And the human gardens of rose-lip girls,
And all the pageant that waits the call
As the toe drives into the waiting ball.

But leave me the halfback's driving might,
The surging lines in a bitter fight,
The sweat and smear of the warring soul
As the tackle opens a two-foot hole;
The roar of the crowds, with their breasts aflame,
The ringing cheers, with their eddying swirls,
The interference, the deadly pass,
The grip and crash of the swirling mass.

For the crowd fades out and the cheers dip low
When the fourth down comes, with a yard to go.
And in the struggle along the field
The battle changes to sword and shield
And the knightly tourneys that used to be
In the golden era of chivalry.

The world grows soft as the years advance
Further and further from sword and lance,
When the caveman, after his morning's fun,
Slew the mammoth and mastodon;
But his ghost at the gridiron calls through space:
"These, too, are worthy to build a race."

The trouble with the future is that it usually arrives before we are ready for it.

It is becoming more and more apparent that we rust out instead of wear out. Physical and mental activity are vital if we wish to prolong the youthful portion of life and enjoy later years.

A player's mind, like his or her body, must be in condition.

The team player is the most valuable player on the team.

Anyone who stops learning is old, whether this happens at 20 or 80.

–Henry Ford

If you know it, show it!

Half of being smart is knowing what you're dumb at.

You cannot do a kindness too soon because you never know how soon it will be too late.

–Ralph Waldo Emerson

Set your goal higher than you can reach—then reach it.

–Glenn Steward

We can often do more for others by correcting our own faults than by trying to correct theirs.

Tip to Young Fighters

Pardon me, I don't want to bore you, you and your half dizzy mates, but look at the field out before you where there's "a million" that waits. "The million" I mention is money, it's yours for a hook and a jab, for high-grade condition, offensive ignition, and maybe a right-fisted stab.

Pardon, you kids who are swinging the leather in clubs here and there. Mugs who are too often clinging to less than a dollar to spare. Those whom the flophouse is dating, all written down in the book, look, there's a million that's waiting for only a jab and a hook.

In My Dream…

I heard some high school teachers cry: "What did they learn in junior high?" But those who teach the seventh grade a different explanation made: "The grade schools simply don't succeed: They never teach them how to read." Each grade school teacher says, "Oh dear, what did they teach 'em all last year?" In first grade with contempt, sublime, we say: "Kindergarten is a mess because parents have failed with readiness." Ah me! The day is almost here, with needles and new pills every year we'll brave the pregnant mother's wrath, and inject pre-natal science and math.

A certain amount of monotony is essential to life. Those who always seek to flee monotony are cutting themselves off from the life-giving force of renewal. It is the monotony of the sun's rising each morning that makes variety possible.

A ship in a harbor is safe, but that is not what ships are built for.

If

If you can keep your head when all about you
Are losing theirs and blaming it on you;
If you can trust yourself when all men doubt you,
But make allowance for their doubting too:
If you can wait and not be tired by waiting,
Or, being lied about, don't deal in lies,
Or being hated don't give way to hating,
And yet don't look too good, nor talk too wise;

If you can dream—and not make your dreams your master;
If you can think—and not make thoughts your aim,
If you can meet with Triumph and Disaster
And treat those two imposters just the same:
If you can bear to hear the truth you've spoken
Twisted by knaves to make a trap for fools,
Or watch the things you gave your life to, broken,
And stoop and build 'em up with worn-out tools;

If you can make one heap of all your winnings
And risk it on one turn of pitch-and-toss,
And lose, and start again at your beginnings,
And never breathe a word about your loss:
If you can force your heart and nerve and sinew
To serve your turn long after they are gone,
And so hold on when there is nothing in you
Except the Will, which says to them: "Hold on!"

If you can talk with crowds and keep your virtue,
Or walk with Kings—nor lose the common touch,
If neither foes nor loving friends can hurt you,
If all men count with you, but none too much:
If you can fill the unforgiving minute
With sixty seconds' worth of distance run,
Yours is the Earth and everything that's in it,
And-which is more—you'll be a Man, my son!

—Rudyard Kipling

The darkest hour in the history of any young man is when he sits down to study how to get money without honestly earning it.

–Horace Greeley

It is more than probable that the average man could, with no injury to his health, increase his efficiency fifty percent.

–Walter Dill Scott

Dear kid:

Today you asked me for a job. From the look of your shoulders as you walked out, I suspect you've been turned down before, and maybe you believe by now that kids out of high school can't find work.

But, I hired a teenager today. You saw him. He was the one with polished shoes and a necktie. What was so special about him? Not experience: Neither of you had any. It was his attitude that put him on the payroll instead of you. Attitude, son, a-t-t-i-t-u-d-e. He wanted that job badly enough to shuck the leather jacket, get a haircut, and look in the phone book to find out what this company makes. He did his best to impress me. That's where he edged you out.

You see, kid, people who hire people aren't "with" a lot of things. We know more about bingo than Ringo, and we have some stone-age ideas about who owes whom a living. Maybe that makes us prehistoric, but there's nothing wrong with the checks we sign, and if you want one you'd better tune to our wavelength.

Ever hear of empathy? It's the trick of seeing the other fellow's side of things. What I needed was someone who'd go out in the plant, keep his eyes open, and work for me like he'd work for himself. If you have even the vaguest idea of what I'm trying to say, let it show the next time you ask for a job. You'll be head and shoulders above the rest.

It takes a hammer of practice to drive the nail of success.

Unless you try to do something beyond what you have already done and mastered, you will never grow.

There is no substitute for hard work and effort beyond the call of mere duty. That is what strengthens the soul and ennobles one's character.

–Walter Camp

Give up trying to know everything, to embrace all. Learn to limit yourself, to content yourself with some definite thing, and some definite work; dare to be what you are, and to learn to resign with a good grace all that you are not, and to believe in your own individuality.

–Amiel

People often say that a person has not yet found himself; but the self is not something that one finds. It is something one creates.

The most valuable result of all education is the ability to make yourself do the thing you have to do, when it has to be done, whether you like it or not.

This is the true joy in life: being used for a purpose recognized by yourself as a mighty one, being thoroughly worn out before you are thrown on the scrap heap, being a force of nature instead of a feverish, selfish little clot of ailments and grievances complaining that the world will not devote itself to making you happy.

–Bernard Shaw

Learn as if you were to live forever.
Live as if you were to die tomorrow.

Teaching students to count is not as important as teaching them what counts.

Education might not make you a leader, but it should teach you which leader to follow.

Those who don't read have no advantage over those who can't.

We need to think more about earning money and less about taking it.

–Lewis Wiznitzi

What you are to be you are now becoming.

If you are average, you are as close to the bottom as you are to the top.

If you want a place in the sun, you must expect some blisters.

Christianity is a roll-up-your-sleeves religion, not a sit-back-and-watch one.

Boy Wanted

WANTED! Boys who'll bide their time, and wait the hills of life to climb, boys out of school who do not seek a grown man's wages in a week, and will not sell the future years for some small gain which now appears; bright, eager boys who want to learn and work for more than what they earn.

BOYS WANTED of a rugged stock, who will not daily watch the clock; ambitious boys, alert to see wherever they can useful be; boys who are not inclined to shirk, but put their hearts into their work and go to tasks which must be done as though it were their greatest fun.

BOYS WANTED—not the flabby kind that seem some easy post to find; not careless boys who think the boss is rich enough to suffer loss, but the boys who think and work and train for that promotion they may gain, and for that job ahead prepare—such boys are wanted everywhere.

–Gen. Douglas MacArthur

One worthwhile task carried to a successful conclusion is worth half-a-hundred half-finished tasks.

Duty is a very personal thing. It is what comes from knowing the need to take action and not just a need to urge others to do something.

The number of people who don't take advantage of their talents is more than made up for by the number who take advantage of talents they scarcely have.

A person should have enough education so she doesn't have to look up to anyone. She should also have enough to be wise enough not to look down on anyone.

Education is what you get from reading the small print on a contract. Experience is what you get from not reading it.

Shortchange your education now and you may be short of change the rest of your life.

Bring Your Children Up or Down

To bring down your children:

*   Let them have plenty of spending money.

*   Permit them to choose their own companions without restraint or direction.

*   Give them a latchkey and allow them to return home late at night.

*   Make no inquiry as to where and with whom they spend their leisure moments.

*   Give them to understand that manners make a good substitute for morals.

*   Teach them to expect pay for every act of helpfulness to others.

*   Let them spend Sunday hours, between services, on the street.

*   Be careful never to let them hear your voice in prayer for their salvation and spiritual growth.

To bring up your children:

*   Make home the brightest and most attractive place on earth.

*   Make them responsible for the performance of a limited number of daily duties.

*   Never punish them in anger.

*   Do not ridicule their conceits, but rather talk frankly on matters in which they are interested.

*   Let them feel free to invite their friends to your home and table.

*   Be careful to impress upon their mind that building character is more important than making money.

*   Live Christ before them all the time, then you will be able to talk Christ to them with power.

*   Be much in prayer for their salvation and spiritual growth.

It may be true that to err is human, but to remain in error is stupid.

Time Bank

Let's suppose that you had a bank that each morning credited your account with $1440, with one condition: Whatever part you had failed to use during the day would be erased from your account, no balance to be carried over.

What would you do? You'd draw out every cent every day and use it to the best advantage. Well, you do have such a bank, and its name is TIME. Every morning it credits you with 1440 minutes. It writes off as forever lost whatever portion of this you have failed to invest to good purpose. There is no drawing against tomorrow.

Consider the Hammer—

It keeps its head.
It doesn't fly off the handle.
It keeps pounding away.
It finds the point and then drives it home.
It looks at the other side, too, and thus often clinches the matter.
It makes mistakes, but when it does, it starts all over.
It is the only knocker in the world that does any good.

Once, to every being and nation, comes a moment to decide in the strife between truth and falsehood for the good or evil.

Nothing gives a person so much advantage over another as to remain cool and unruffled under all circumstances.

It's Never a Mistake...

...to tell a person how clever or smart or interesting she is...to say, "I don't know," if you really don't...to ask the advice of an expert...to inquire about grandchildren...to take the time and trouble to put another person at ease...to listen politely to a child...to guess a person's age as five years under what it possibly could be...to praise your husband or wife for the qualities you most want him or her to have...to let the hosts know you had fun...to say "I'm sorry," even when the other person is wrong...to tell someone you value her opinion...to say something nice to the next person you meet...to tell a parent something complimentary about his child.

—Inspiration

Advice

- Beware of enterprises that require new clothes. (Thoreau)
- Do not gamble with anyone who has a city for a first name.
- If you had everything you wanted, where would you put it? (Steven Wright)
- Life is not simple.
- The world is full of right answers to bad questions.
- The test of a first rate intelligence is the ability to hold two opposed ideas in the mind at the same time and still function. (F. Scott Fitzgerald)

—Richard T. Goode, Vital-Speeches

The most powerful KING on earth is Wor-KING; The laziest KING on earth is Shir-KING; One of the worst KINGs is Smo-KING; The Wittiest KING on earth is Jo-KING; The quietest KING on earth is Thin-KING; The thirstiest KING is Drin-KING; The slyest KING is Win-KING; And the noisiest KING is Tal-KING.

My grandfather once told me that there are two kinds of people: those who do the work and those who take the credit. He told me to try to be in the first group; there was much less competition there.

My Creed

To live as gently as I can;
To be, no matter where, a human;
To take what comes of good or ill
And cling to faith and honor still;
To do my best, and let that stand
The record of my brain and hand;
And then, should failure come to me,
Still work and hope for victory.
To have no secret place wherein
I stoop unseen to shame or sin
To be the same when I'm alone
And when my every deed is known;
To live undaunted and unafraid
Of any step that I have made;
To be without pretense or shame
Exactly what men think I am.
To leave some simple mark behind
To keep my having lived in mind;
If enmity to aught I show,
To be an honest, generous foe,
To play my little part, nor whine
That greater honors are not mine.
This, I believe, is all I need
For my philosophy and creed.

–Edgar Guest

I do my thing, and you do your thing. I am not in this world to live up to your expectations. And you are not in this world to live up to mine.

You are you, and I am me, and if by chance we both can give in a little—we might become friends.

Anyone can carry his burden, however hard, until nightfall. Anyone can do his work, however hard, for one day.

–Robert Louis Stevenson

About the Author

Larry Bielat is an international motivational speaker. He coached football for 35 years at every level—high school, college (University of Colorado, University of New Mexico, Pittsburgh, MSU), and professional (USFL's Philadelphia Stars). The author of several books, Bielat is a former Michigan State University Assistant Alumni Director and radio color analyst for MSU Spartan football.

In high school, Bielat was an All-American quarterback. He lettered three years in football at MSU and was the first quarterback of the New York Jets. He was also offered a baseball contract by the New York Yankees.

Bielat and his wife, Lois Hilden, live in West Bloomfield, MI. They have four children and 11 grandchildren.